PARA-X POWERS
UNLEASH THE PSI WITHIN YOU

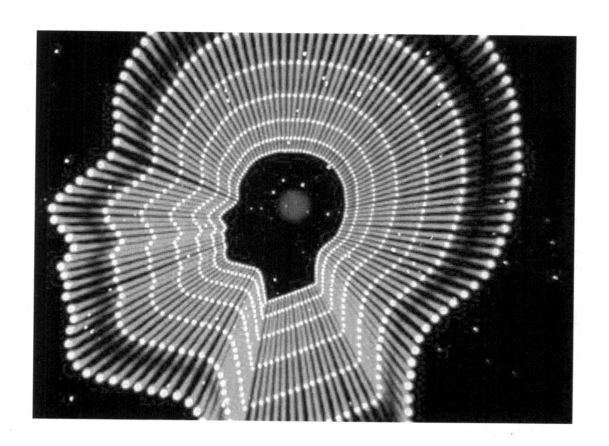

GLOBAL COMMUNICATIONS

PARA-X POWERS

PARA-X POWERS: UNLEASH THE PSI WITHIN YOU

By Dragonstar, Swami Panchadasi, William W. Atkinson, William Oribello,
Tim R. Swartz, Timothy Green Beckley

Timothy Green Beckley: Editorial Director
Carol Rodriguez: Publishers Assistant
Tim Swartz: Associate Editor
Sean Casteel: Editorial Assistant
William Kern: Editorial Assistant
Cover Art: Tim Swartz

1. Dragonstar, Panchadasi, Swami, Atkinson, William, Oribello,
William, Swartz, Tim, Beckley, Timothy, Magical Arts, Metaphysics,
History – Nonfiction

I. Title: Para-X Powers: Unleash the Psi Within You

133'.4

For free catalog write:
Global Communications
P.O. Box 753
New Brunswick, NJ 08903

Free Subscription to Conspiracy Journal E-Mail Newsletter
www.conspiracyjournal.com

PARA-X POWERS

CONTENTS

PARA-X POWERS

PARA-X POWERS

1
THE POWER WITHIN

DID you ever notice that there are some people who seem to always come out ahead in life? You know the ones...they are always at the right time and place to get the very best of everything. They get the best jobs, make a lot of money, are super attractive to the opposite sex, and they make it look so easy. What makes these people especially irritating is that it seems as if they don't try at all for these things that life just tosses everything that they desire right into their laps.

So what is it that makes these people so successful? Hard work? Dumb luck? Trust fund? For some, their success does come from hard work and dumb luck. And of course it doesn't hurt to be born into an already rich and successful family. But we are not talking about these people. We are talking about those who have learned the secrets to make life work for them rather than against them. We are talking about the powerful energies of the Universe that are available to all who are willing to learn how to control them with some very simple techniques.

These powerful universal energies for centuries have been called by many names: Prana, Chi, The Force, and a thousand other names. These are the energies of Creation...but what is not widely known is that these energies did not disappear right after "The Beginning." Creation is a continual process, it never stopped, it is happening right now – it is eternal.

The other secret is that we are all participants in Creation. We all have the ability to harness these creative energies to literally build our reality around us. We do it every second, every minute of our lives. However, most people have no idea that they are the creators, the builders of their lives. They do not realize that their very thoughts are constructing their reality from second to second. For most people this is why their lives are so chaotic and unformed. Their lives are their very thoughts made into reality.

Wouldn't it be nice to learn how to control your thoughts and harness this energy? Wouldn't it be nice to use this energy to get what you want out of life...to obtain your hearts desires? This is what this book is all about, how to control your thoughts and in turn, how to control the creative energies that flow through the Universe, and through all of us.

PARA-X POWERS

PARA-X POWERS

Let us start by giving a name for this energy...let's call it Para-X Powers. Para-X Powers is an actual living force. It is the force that makes plants and animal grow; it is what enables all living things to move and act. It is the force which enables the growing mushroom to rise up the slabs of paving stone—or causes the roots of a tree to split open the great boulders, into the crevices of which they have crept. Para-X Power is not an abstraction or speculative nothing, it is an existent, living, mental, acting force, manifesting sometimes with an appalling power, and sometimes with a delicate, subtle touch that is almost imperceptible, but which accomplishes its purpose.

For centuries, the techniques of Para-X Powers have been taught by Mystery Schools and secret Mystical Orders. These mystical teachings were intended only for the few initiates who dedicated their lives for that particular order or society. Because of this, mystical teachings like Para-X Powers were hidden within a lot of nonsense words, phrases and parables. Only the select few could understand the true meanings hidden within the metaphysical garbage.

Practically every Holy book ever produced was written to be confusing. Look at the Bible for example. It is full of contradictions and vague, meaningless parables. But to the select few who had received the proper teachings, the true esoteric meaning of the Bible is very clear. With the help of some of the worlds leading esoteric researchers, Dragonstar, Swami Panchadasi, Tim R. Swartz, William Walker Atkinson, William Oribello, and Timothy Green Beckley, this book cuts through all of the meaningless metaphysical nonsense and goes directly to the heart of the teachings. Para-X Powers can be used by anyone who is willing to open their mind and believe that they have the power to make dreams come true.

In order to reach a clear conception of the universality of Para-X Power, let us consider its manifestations as we see them, unquestioned, in the Universe on the many planes of life and activity. Beginning with the more familiar instances of its operation and manifestation, let us then proceed to delve still deeper until we reach instances not so easily perceived; and then still further back until we find it in places and in things that are generally regarded as lacking in Para-X Power and life.

And, here let me say that I hold that life and Para-X Power are always found in company with each other – there is some close relationship between the two – they are probably twin-phases of the same thing, or else twin-manifestations of the same underlying reality. There is nothing without life in the Universe. The Universe

PARA-X POWERS

is alive, and has mind and Pará-X Power in every part and particle of itself. This is not an original idea of course, the leading scientific minds admit it today and the Eastern philosophers have known it for thousands of years.

Dr. Caleb Williams Saleeby, in his important scientific work, "Evolution: the Master Key," goes even still further in his claim of a living Universe; and life accompanied by mind and Para-X Powers. He says, among other things: "Life is potential in matter; life-energy is not a thing unique and created at a particular time in the past. If evolution be true, living matter has been evolved by natural processes from matter which is, apparently, not alive. But if life is a potential in matter, it is a thousand times more evident that mind is potential in life. The evolutionist is impelled to believe that mind is potential in matter. The microscopic cell, a minute speck of matter that is to become man, has in it the promise and germ of mind. May we not then draw the inference that the elements of mind are present in those chemical elements, carbon, oxygen, hydrogen, nitrogen, sulphur, phosphorus, sodium, potassium, chlorine – that are found in the cell. Not only must we do so, bat we must go further, since we know that each of these elements, and every other, is built up out of one invariable unit, the electron, and we must there fore assert that mind is potential in the unit of matter – the electron itself."

But we have not as yet reached the utmost limit of scientific investigation regarding the presence of mind and Para-X Powers in the Universe. "Further than the atoms?" you may ask. Yes, further than the atoms. What is true regarding atoms is true of the ions or electrons of which they are composed – these tinier particles are attracted and repelled; form groups and combinations which regulate the kind of atom produced; and manifest the same kind of "affinity" that is noticeable in the atoms. And more than this – these particles, as well as all forms of physical energy, are believed to emerge from the ether, that subtle, tenuous, universal substance, which, although unseen, and intangible, is held to exist in order to account for the phenomena of the Universe.

PARA-X POWERS AND THE LAWS OF ATTRACTION

The law of attraction is the most powerful force in the Universe. It is a law that if worked in harmony with Para-X Powers, can bring you much in the way of blessings and success. If you work against it, it can only bring you pain and misery.

People who are successful know the law of attraction, but not many people know about it. This truth has been hidden for years.

PARA-X POWERS

Very prominent people have kept it hidden for many centuries only because some wanted all the fortune for themselves and did not want to share it. The outcome for these people was catastrophic. It is a known fact that if you knew the Law of Attraction, and acted in accordance with it, you could get anything you wanted in life.

Have you ever heard the old saying "like attracts like"? This is a law that means you attract what you are or vibrate to. So if you vibrate to goodness, goodness comes to you. Another way to look at this is by looking at yourself as energy. Everything in life is energy. Look under a microscope and you will see nothing but small atoms with space all around. And it is constantly moving. Nothing in this Universe stands still. Atoms are constantly in motion. You can't see it but they are there and are in motion.

One form of energy attracts another form of energy. If you look at electrons, you will find one electron, which may be a weaker electron, is attracted to another electron. This is how electrons flow through wires. The universal law of attraction is simple. We attract whatever we choose to give our attention to. It doesn't matter whether it is good or bad. If we focus on bad things, we will attract more bad things.

Ever heard of the expression everything happens in threes? The reason this happens is because when one bad thing happens, you are focusing on that bad thing so another bad thing or event occurs. As long as you focus on anything bad, badness will continue to manifest itself in your life. But the minute you stop focusing on bad and focus in on good, you change the pattern and now good things start coming your way. It doesn't matter who you are or where you live. It doesn't even matter your religion or stature in life. Para-X Powers and the law of attraction are there and they work for everyone. You just have to connect to it.

Do you know you have enough energy in your body to light a city for a month? If you could tap into this, you wouldn't have to pay your electric bill anymore. But the only problem is we are conditioned not to use those resources for the betterment of ourselves. We allow others to control us, tell us what to think, say, or do. If we could harness the power of our minds, we would be invincible. This is why for centuries Para-X Powers have been kept secret from everyone. Imagine what you could achieve if you used one-tenth the power your mind possessed.

For years, we were brainwashed to follow a certain path. We couldn't think for ourselves. We had to just live day-by-day and solve problems as they came up. We couldn't use our creative mind to do the things we truly wanted to do. We were told that life was off limits and that we had to do what we were told or pay the consequences. Ever wonder why this world is so screwed up now?

PARA-X POWERS

It is because we have been inhibited for so long. If we knew Para-X Powers and applied it in our lives daily, we would have so much power and control that it would be scary.

When we live by others standards and just float along from day to day, we are creating that type of world for ourselves. We are vibrating that way for ourselves. We are attracting that type of lifestyle, that type of way of living. But if we turned that around and started living the life we wanted, focused on the good things in life and really applied the law of attraction in every aspect of our lives, we would be superhuman creatures with the ability to command the world. We could literally have what we wanted, and when we wanted it. We would have total control of our lives.

In fact, if you are sitting down right now, think for a minute about a magnet. If you do not have one nearby, close your eyes and imagine one. Notice when you take a magnet and hold it close to metal, the metal is attracted to that magnet. What power right? That magnet literally grabbed and pulled that metal to itself. Imagine what you could do if you were like a magnet. But you know what? You are a magnet. Scientists have conducted much research on the brain and found there are neuro-transmitters in the brain that send signals from one stem and cell to another. These are electrical impulses that travel from the brain to the spinal cord, sending electrical impulses to the muscles in our body, forcing those muscles to move according to the way we want them. Because of this discovery, we now know that we have the ability to attract what we want by just using our mind. We attract because we are a part of the Creative Force. Therefore, if you realize your part in the creation of your reality and use that power, you can accomplish anything that you want.

This is why when you think about scarcity, you get more scarcity. If you think about love, you get more love. If you think about abundance, you get more abundance. It happens. This is how Para-X Powers and the law of attraction works. And to work in contradiction to it can only prove fatal at most.

Therefore, if you think of yourself as a powerful attractor, and you use this god-given gift, you will attract more of what you want in your life, simply by thinking about it, then acting on it. However, there is one thing you need to know here. There is one ingredient you cannot leave out or the law of attraction won't work. You must not just think of what you want, you must also feel it. Put emotion behind it. Then when you put emotion behind it, take action by executing your desires and the actions you take will go out to the Universe, which in turn will give you your results. It happens every time no matter what we think about.

PARA-X POWERS

Now someone may say, "I thought things come from our heart." Actually you are right. They do. Our heart is the seed of emotions. When we think of an object in our mind, we then send that image to our heart and act on it with emotion. This emotion we feel then forces us to take action. This is why, in a way, we do think from our heart. After we think of what we want from our mind, our heart takes over and sends out to the universe what we want and the Universe responds.

A formula makes this principle easy to follow. If we want something in our lives, the first thing we do is think it. After we think it for a while (and this means placing images in our mind), we then transfer this to our heart, where we act on our thinking with feelings. Feelings we know are emotions. So when we feel something, we are using our emotions. After we have a deeply engrained feeling over the image or thought, we then act on that thought and feeling by taking action. When we take the necessary action, the Universe shows up and gives us the results we wanted.

But we must act in harmony with it. We cannot just think, feel, and act only one time. We must live for the result every second of everyday. We must consciously and even subconsciously think about it everyday. Like I said earlier, when you think and act on what you want, you must vibrate toward it for your desires to be fulfilled.

THE THREE STEPS TOWARDS PARA-X POWERS

To begin to learn how to develop your Para-X Powers you need to consider the three steps. Para-X Powers work by performing three steps. And these steps must be done in order for the process to work. These steps are:

1. Getting clear. You must know what it is you want or else you won't get it. If you don't know what it is you want, the Universe won't know either.

2. Vibrate to the level of energy corresponding to what you want. If you want something and you think on it, feel it, and act on it, you must keep that level of energy going until you achieve the results you are after.

3. Attract what you want like a magnet. If you focus on what you want but don't allow it to come into your life, it won't. You have to be willing to accept it and acknowledge it. Then when you act, it will occur.

PARA-X POWERS

This whole idea of attraction does work. You just have to practice it everyday. And since we are creatures of habit, when we get a hold on something and practice everyday, we develop it into a habit. This then becomes automatic. The law of attraction can become the same thing. If you use it everyday, on a regular basis, and practice it this way, you will eventually, in a short period, find that it becomes a habit that you will subconsciously practice.

Para-X Powers are working in your life right now but you may not be aware of it or notice it. Whatever you do during the course of a day, whatever thoughts you think about, you are attracting. It is as simple as that. Think about it. You sometimes run across people in your life who tell you that something happened in their lives, something wonderful and they celebrate because they believe they attracted it. Do you know what I mean? But what about those people who seem to get what they refer to as bad luck. They always cry "Why me?" "Why is this so?" The answer is: because they attracted it. They vibrated to it, which caused it to happen. The first step to getting what you want is to own it or accept accountability for what you asked for.

Of course, there are those who wonder why they ask for one thing, but don't get it. This is because your vibrations or energy wasn't tuned into what you wanted. Remember, the law of attraction is you get what you think of. It has no distinction as to what is real or imagined. It doesn't know what is meant to be or not. It doesn't know whether you should have it or you shouldn't. It only responds to what you wish for and gives it to you.

How can you use Para-X Powers? How can you practice it? What steps do you need to take to use it? You may not believe it, but the steps you need to take are easy. But you must do them, believe in them and believe in yourself, or they will not work. So are you ready to get tuned into the universe and get clear? Are you ready to work in harmony with Para-X Powers and the laws of the Universe and become successful? If so here are the steps you need to follow:

1. Get clear. You must know exactly what it is you want. If you are in doubt, vague, or too general, you won't get anywhere. You must know exactly what it is you want first. Only then will you be able to focus and concentrate on that thought.

2. Visualize what you want and vibrate to it. You must form a mental image in your mind so you can see it as if you had it in your possession. You must understand what it is you are seeing and look at it as if you can touch it. When you visualize it, you have to

vibrate to it. Don't just see the image, feel it, touch it, let it become part of you. If it is a woman you want, visualize the woman you are looking for. Picture her hair color. See how tall she is. Notice her facial features. Visualize yourself holding her, hugging her, or even kissing her. Then transfer this image to your heart and use your feelings to convey how you feel about this woman. For women, you can do the same for a man. Repeat the same process, the only difference is you will be looking at a man instead of a woman. Regardless of your sexual preference, you just have to visualize the person in front of you and see him/her as being there with you and experience the joy of that person in your presence.

3. Now allow it to be a part of you. You can allow it by simply agreeing to it and say yes to the idea that you want it. When you do this, you are in fact allowing it to come to you. If you visualize receiving a check for $1000, picture yourself accepting it while saying "yes" and "thank you." Hold it like it is yours. Embrace it. Tell the universe you acknowledge it and want it. Tell the universe "thank you for giving it to me" and then accept it. This way you are allowing it to enter your life.

4. Take action to fulfill your request. You must work in harmony with what you wish and do so without wavering. You must make a concerted effort to always dwell on wanting it. By doing so, you will attract it without any obstacles in your path. Remember, when you think, you then feel. After you feel, you take action. This action gives you your results. It works every time, no exceptions.

USE PARA-X POWERS IN BUSINESS

The above steps will help you to become better attractors. But you can also apply Para-X Powers in your business life as well. How? Here are some ways you can use Para-X Powers in your business dealings:

- Identify your prospects: What you do here is simply list what you want in your ideal customer. Keep writing down everything you can think of that you want to see in the type of customer you want. Then think on this list in your mind.

- Vibrate on them: Instead of vibrating on the bad customers you may have gotten in the past, vibrate on those customers you want to see from the list you have written down and are now in your mind. Continue to vibrate and add feelings to the vibrations.

- Follow through: When you start getting calls or making calls, and you have selected each client from those calls, celebrate that you have attained the client you were looking for. Keep doing this for each client that matched the list you made up. Pour your thoughts, emotions, feelings, and energy into that list and you will find the right clients will come knocking on your door, begging for your business.

- Celebration time: After you have completed the list of clients and attained the amount of clients you want for now, celebrate the moment with acceptance. Look at yourself, give yourself a big hug, and say "I did it. I attracted these people. I am what made it possible to have these great clients. I created these clients with my intent. These clients came to me because of Para-X Powers."

- Get a bragging buddy: While you celebrate your success, find a buddy or friend who also celebrated attracting something or someone good in his or her life and celebrate together. Brag about it to each other. Acknowledge each other's achievements.

- Keep a log: As you accomplish your feat and win new clients, keep a log of your success and how Para-X Powers worked in your life and present moment. Do this each time a new client comes on board. This way you can keep track of the methods you used so you can repeat them over and over again.

- Review customer or client list: Every week review your client or customer list to see who you have on their and how many of them actually relate to your wants and desires. If you find a client or customer who doesn't match your requirements any longer, remove them and using the steps you used to create the original clients, put the process in motion and create more clients to replace the ones you removed.

When you use Para-X Powers, you do not worry about where it is coming from or how you will get it. The Universe will take care of those details. All you do is your part and the Universe will do its part. You cannot have any doubts as to your ability to get

PARA-X POWERS

what you want. You must have strong assurance that you will get what you asked for no matter what. If you have any doubts, you cancel out your request and won't get anything. So, always focus on it and never have any doubts about what you ask for. The Universe is very giving. All you have to do is act in accordance with it, vibrate to it, and work along with it, and everything your heart desires will be yours.

Para-X Power and the Law of Attraction are very powerful and forceful in the way they work. You can just think it, act on it, and bingo, it happens. But what would be even better is if you were to focus on an exact thing, event, or person you want in your thoughts. For example, let's say your goal is to marry a beautiful blond woman. You wouldn't just visualize any type of blond woman. You would visualize a blond woman with certain characteristics. You would want to visualize whether she wears glasses or not. You want to visualize the way she wears her hair. Is it straight or curly? You want to be as specific as possible with your intent.

What if you wanted a certain amount of money? Visualize you getting a check for $10,000 dollars. Or maybe you want to go higher. Or perhaps you want to go lower? You know what you want. But you have to gear your mind so you can vibrate to it. Otherwise, if you aren't clear as to what you want, the Universe won't know and will send you money that may not be enough for your needs. So think about that the next time you desire money in your life. As was stated above and before, Para-X Power works. You just have to accept it, act on it, and be in harmony with it. Do this and you can have anything you want.

PARA-X POWERS

We are a part of the same Creative Force that created the Universe. Therefore, if you realize your part in the day by day creation of your reality and use that power, you can accomplish anything that you want.

2
PARA-VISUALIZATION

TO learn how to develop your Para-X Powers, you first have to learn how to effectively utilize the powers of your mind. One key step in this process is learning how to properly visualize what it is that you desire. Every thought is patterned after the mental image that predominates at the time the thought is created. Thoughts are things. Every thought produces an effect on mind and body, and that the effect is always similar to the cause. According to these facts we can therefore produce any effect desired upon mind or body by producing the necessary thought or mental state, so that when we have learned to control our thinking we can control practically everything else in life, because in the last analysis it is thinking that constitutes the one great cause in the life of the individual.

To control thinking, however, we must understand the process of thought creation. To think is to create thought, and to control thinking is to create any thought we like at any time and under any circumstance. When we analyze the process of thinking we find three factors involved; that is, the pattern, the mental substance and the creative energy. The pattern is always the deepest impression, the clearest image, or the predominating idea.

The quality of the mental substance improves with the quality of the mind; and the quantity increases with the expansion of consciousness, while the creative energies grow stronger the less energy we lose and the more we awaken the greater powers from within.

When an idea or image is impressed upon the mind the mental energies will proceed to create thought just like that image; and will continue while that image occupies a permanent position in consciousness. When the mind is very active a great deal of thought is created every second, though the amount varies with the activity of the mind. It is therefore more detrimental for an active mind to think wrong thought than for a mind that is dull or stupid; proving the fact that responsibility always increases as we rise in the scale. It is the function of the creative energies of the mind to create thought that is just like every image impressed upon mind and to continue to create thought in the likeness of that image while it lasts. The creative energies do this of their own accord and we cannot stop them. But we can make them weak or strong, or give them better patterns.

Mind is an art gallery of many pictures, but only the most prominent are selected for models in thought creation. Only those pictures that are sufficiently distinct to be seen by consciousness without special effort are brought before the creative energies as patterns. We thus find that the art of controlling one's thinking and the power to determine what kind of thought is to be created is acquired largely through the training of the mind to impress deeply only such mental pictures as are desired as models for thinking. The law, however, is very simple because as the picture in the mind happens to be at this moment so will also be the thoughts created at this moment, and the mental pictures are in each case the ideas and impressions that we permit in mind.

Whatever enters the mind through the senses can impress the mind, and the result will be a picture or mental image that will become a pattern for the creative energies. What takes shape and form in your mind through your own interior thinking will also impress the mind and become an image or pattern. It is therefore possible through this law to determine what kind of thoughts you are to create by impressing your mind with your own ideas regardless of what environment may suggest to you through your senses, and it is by exercising this power that you place the destiny of body, mind and soul absolutely in your own hands.

As we proceed with this process we find another vital law that may be stated as follows: What we constantly picture upon the mind we shall eventually realize in actual life. This law may be spoken of as a twin sister to the one stated above as they are found to work together in almost every process of thought creation and thought expression.

The one declares that all thought is patterned after the predominating mental pictures while the other declares that the entire external life of man is being daily recreated in the likeness of those mental pictures. The fact is, as the mental tendencies are, so is thought; as thought is, so is character; and it is the combined action of character, ability and purpose that determines what we are to attain or accomplish, or what is to happen to us.

YOUR THOUGHTS ARE REAL

Through Para-X Powers and the Law of Attraction, we see that our thoughts are reality. The external world is a reflection of our internal world. The self constitutes the magnet, and like attracts like. This self who constitutes the magnet is composed of all the active forces, desires, tendencies, motives, states and thoughts that are at work in mind or personality. When we look at everything that is alive throughout our whole being and put all those things together we have what may be termed our present active self. And this self invariably attracts in the external world such conditions as correspond to its own nature. This self and all its parts in the person correspond to the thoughts that we have been creating in mind. In fact the nature of the self is actually composed of thought, mental states and mental activities. We realize, therefore, that when we change our thought, the nature of the self will change, and this change will be good or otherwise depending upon the change of thought.

Your external life is the exact counterpart of this active self. This self is the exact likeness of your thought, and your thoughts are patterned after the pictures that are impressed upon your mind. Therefore we understand that whatever is pictured in the mind will be realized in external life. And the reason why is not only simply explained but can be proven along strictly scientific lines. However, to determine through the law of mind picturing what our external life is to be, every process of mind picturing which we desire to carry out must be continued for a sufficient length of time to give the creative processes the opportunity to make over the whole self.

When a certain picture is formed in the mind thought will be created in the likeness of that picture. This thought goes out and permeates the entire self and changes the self to a degree. But as a rule it takes some time to change the entire self; therefore we must continue to hold the desired picture in mind until the whole self has been entirely made over and has become just like the ideal picture. And you can easily discern when the self has been wholly changed because as soon as the self is changed everything in your life changes. Then a new self will attract new people, new conditions, new environments, new opportunities and new states of being. It is evident therefore that so long as there is no change in the outer life we may know that the self has not been changed. However, the changing process may be going on, but the new has not as yet become stronger than the old, and for the time being things continue as they were.

When the self has been changed to such an extent that the new becomes positive and the old negative we will begin to attract new things. We may therefore begin to attract new and better things for some time before the entire self has been completely changed. When we are changing only a part of the self that part will begin to attract the new while those parts of the self that have not been changed will continue to attract the old as usual. This explains why some people continue to attract trouble and adversity for a while after they have begun to live a larger and a better life.

In promoting the art of mind picturing we must not change ideas or plans at too frequent intervals for such changes will neutralize what has been gained thus far and here is the place where a great many people fail. The average person who wishes to change his life for the better does not hold on to his ideals long enough; that is, he does not give them a fair chance to work themselves out and bring the expected results.

When he does not receive results as soon as he expects he changes his plans and produces new pictures upon the mind. Thus he begins all over again, losing what he had built up through previous plans; but before long becomes discouraged once more, so tries still other ideas or methods. When our ideals are the highest we know we do not have to change them. They cannot be improved upon until we have so entirely recreated ourselves that we can live in a superior state of consciousness. It is therefore highly important to determine positively upon the ideals that we wish to realize, and to hold on to those ideals until they are realized regardless of what may happen in the meantime.

However, we must not infer that we can realize in the external the correspondence of every picture that we hold in mind, because the majority of the mental pictures that we form are so constituted that they can be worked out in practical action. We must therefore distinguish between such ideals, as can be made practical now and those that are simply temporary dreams, having no connection with real life here and now.

KNOW WHAT YOU WANT

To be realized a mental picture must be constant, but only such pictures can be constant as are sufficiently elaborate to involve a complete transformation in yourself, and that are so high that they can act as an inspiration until all your present ideals are realized. When we form such pictures in the mind and continue to hold on to them until they are externally realized we shall certainly obtain the desired realization. At such times we can proceed with the perfect faith that what we have pictured will become true in actual life in days to come, and those days will not be far away. But to use this law the mind must never waver; it must hitch its wagon to a star and never cut the traces.

With Para-Visualization, The idea is to picture all the essentials, that is, all those parts that are distinct or individualized. But we need not include such things as are naturally attracted by the essentials. In other words, apply the law, and that which will naturally come through the application of that law, will be realized.

If you wish to realize a more perfect body it is not necessary to picture the exact physical appearance of that body. You may not know at present what a perfect body should look like. Therefore

19

picture only the quality of perfection in every part of the physical form and those qualities will develop and express themselves more and more throughout your personality. And if you wish to enter a different environment do not give your thought to some special locality, nor to persons and things that would necessarily be included in such an environment. Persons come and go and things are generally the way we wish them to be.

To proceed realize what constitutes an ideal environment and hold that picture in your mind. In analyzing an ideal environment we would find it to contain harmony, beauty, love, peace, joy, desirable opportunities, advantages, ideal friends, wholesome conditions and an abundance of the best of everything that the welfare of human life may require. Therefore we should picture those things and continue to hold them in mind with the faith that we will soon find an environment containing all those things in the highest degree of perfection. Gradually we shall find more and more of them coming into our life until we shall find an environment that comes up in every respect to our ideal.

The law of Para-Visualization can also be effective in changing physical conditions. Any physical malady must eventually disappear if we continue to hold in mind a perfect picture of health and wholeness.

Many have eliminated chronic ailments in a few weeks and even in a few days by this method, and all would succeed if they never pictured disease but perfect health only. In the field of achievement we will find the same facts to hold good. Whenever we fear that we shall not succeed we bring forth the wrong picture, thus the wrong thoughts are created and wrong conditions are produced; in consequence the very thing we feared comes upon us. When we are positively determined to succeed, however, we picture the idea of success and attainment upon the mind, and, according to the law, success will be realized in external life.

Mental and spiritual attainments respond remarkably to Para-Visualization, principally because all true Para-Visualization draws consciousness up into the world of superiority. The same is true in the field of talent. If there is any talent that you wish to develop draw mental pictures of yourself in full possession of that talent and you will comply with the requirements of the steady growth of that talent. This method alone will accomplish much, but when it is associated with our processes of development the results desired will surely be remarkable.

In the building of character, Para-Visualization is of exceptional importance. If you continue to associate only with impure minds and continue to think only of deeds of darkness you will picture only the wrong upon your mind. Thus your thoughts will become wrong and wrong thoughts lead to wrong actions.

The contrary, however, is also true. So therefore if we wish to perfect our conduct we must impress upon the mind only such ideas as will inspire us with desires and aims for greater and higher things.

We live in a world filled strife and danger. For thousands of years we have fought for our lives and the lives of our children and children's children. Everyday we faced death that came at us from every direction. We were born into a world that seemed as if its only desire was to kill us as quickly as possible.

This is the world that we evolved in; centuries of this sort of life made a deep impression upon humanity. Our brains developed in ways that enabled us to handle the demands our dangerous world had thrust upon us.

There was little time to contemplate the immaterial, the spiritual part of us. If our ancestors sat for too long, reflecting on the mysteries of our universe, they soon found themselves victims of some hungry predator.

It is no wonder that humanity has become so obsessed with the material world and all of its pleasures and perils. We can hardly thrust the finger of blame at our fellows when they hunger for immediate physical gratification and desire to obtain riches and shiny gee-gaws.

This obsession with the material, however, is merely a remnant of our former, primitive existence. It no longer serves any true purpose in our overall survival...it is vestigial. Yet, it remains the single most driving force of our lives.

It is time to throw these useless desires away and leave our primitive beginnings behind. It is time to embrace the spiritual beings that occupy our bodies of clay and understand our place, our participation within the universe.

It is time to realize that we are all GODS.

PARA-X POWERS

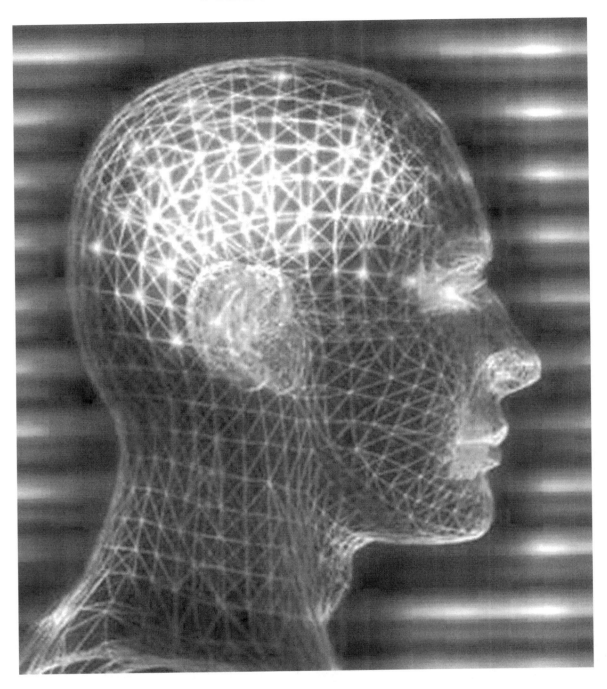

When a certain picture is formed in the mind thought will be created in the likeness of that picture. This thought goes out and permeates the entire self and changes the self to a degree.

PARA-X POWERS

I THINK, THEREFORE I AM

We all admit that character can be influenced most decidedly by Para-Visualization, but everybody may not be ready to accept the idea that ability, attainment, achievement, environment and destiny can be affected in the same way. However, it is only a full analysis of the law of mind picturing that is necessary to prove this also to be an exact scientific fact. It is the way we think that determines the quality of the mind, and it is the quality of the mind that determines what our ability, mental capacity and mental force is to be. And we can readily understand that the improvement of ability will naturally be followed by increase in attainment and achievement as well as a greater control over fate and destiny.

Man is constantly increasing his ability, is making his own future and is making that future brighter and greater every day. Therefore, if mind pictures can affect mental quality, mental power and mental ability they can also affect environment and achievement, and in brief, the entire external life of man. In looking for evidence for the fact that mental pictures can affect ability, simply compare results from efforts that are inspired by high ideals and efforts that are inspired by low ideals and you have all the evidence you need.

When your mind is filled with pictures of superiority you will think superior thoughts...Thoughts that have more quality, power and worth, and such thoughts cannot fail to give power, quality and worth to your talents and faculties. We also find that tendencies, desires and motives originate largely from mental pictures and we also know that these factors exercise an enormous power in life. The active self of man is so dominated by desires and tendencies that it is absolutely impossible to change the self until tendencies and desires are changed. But tendencies and desires as well as motives cannot be changed without changing the mental pictures -a fact of extreme importance.

With Para-Visualization you can create or eliminate any kind of desire; you can produce or remove any tendency that you like. All that is necessary is to impress upon the mind the perfect picture of a desire or tendency that you wish and then continue to hold that picture in the mind until you have results. A mental picture, however, is not necessarily something that you can see in the same way as you see external, tangible things. It is an impression or idea or concept and is seen only by the understanding. In order to hold a mental picture constantly in mind keep all the essentials of that picture before your attention; that is, try to be conscious of the real nature of those powers and possibilities that are represented by the picture. In other words, enter into the very nature of those qualities which that picture represents.

The mind is very large. It is therefore possible to form mental pictures of as many ideals as we like, but at first it is best to choose only a few. Begin by picturing a perfect body, an able mind, a strong character and a beautiful soul; after that an ideal interior life and an ideal external environment. Thus you have the foundation of a great life, a rich life and a wonderful life. Keep these pictures constantly before your mind. In fact, train yourself to actually live for those pictures. And you will find all things in your life-changing daily to become more and more like those pictures. In the course of time you will realize in actual life the exact likeness of those pictures; that is, what you have constantly pictured upon your mind you will realize in actual life. Then you can form new and more beautiful pictures to be realized in like manner as you build for a still greater future.

3
PARA-CONCENTRATION

THE power of Para-Concentrated thinking is an important key in being able to master your Para-X Powers. We all have the ability to concentrate effectively. However, the average man does not use even a fraction of that power properly. Most people are not the masters of their minds, and to put an end to this undesirable condition is one of the first and foremost aims of this study of concentration. The proper control of a machine means that we are able to put it into action, modify its speed and finally to stop it when needed. This is just what is required of a disciplined mind.

True concentration is not merely an ability to direct and maintain our full and exclusive attention for some minutes on, say, a match-head; but rather it is the ability to stop the thinking machine and look at it when it has ceased revolving. A craftsman feels sure that his hands will obey him and execute the exact movements he requires. Anyway, he does not even think about it and works without worrying whether or not his hands will do just what he wants at a given moment.

Under such conditions hands and other human organs, when working properly, constitute a harmonious unit, capable of functioning in their own particular sphere of action. Imagine now that some part of your body refuses to obey the impulses issued from the control center of your brain. And for example, instead of pouring a glass of water when you are thirsty, your hand lights a cigarette or even refuses to move at all. Then surely you will consider that such a hand is of little use.

Now look closely at the functions of your mind-brain. Can you affirm with utter certainty that you are always thinking when and only about what you really want to and that therefore you know from where your thoughts and feelings are coming into the light of your consciousness? Can you withhold the entry or limit the duration of thoughts in your mind for as long as you wish? If you are able to analyze your thinking processes, a sincere answer will always be in the negative.

So it would seem that the average person is not a good craftsman, because he cannot control his chief tool, the mind and its thoughts. His life is spent on using and accepting something which originates beyond his reach and understanding. The practical study of Para-Concentration opens to us not only the world of results, but also of causes, and this lifts us beyond the slavery of uncontrolled feelings and thoughts.

PARA-X POWERS

DIRECTING YOUR PARA-X POWERS

An amazing example illustrating the direct influence of Para-Concentrated human willpower on matter is that of a needle turning in a glass of water. Mme H. P. Blavatsky used this to train her disciple, Annie Besant, and to test the results of that training in concentration.

Place a small needle in a glass of water and to prevent it sinking, cover with a thin layer of grease by smearing your fingers with a little oil or butter and passing the needle between them. It should then be lowered carefully and slowly onto the surface of the water so that it floats freely in the middle without touching the sides.

Sit facing the glass with your chin cupped in your palms, elbows supporting them and resting on top of a table. Then when the needle is lying quietly on the surface, gaze at it intently with a strong desire to turn it by the sheer force of your will, centered on it as if imaginary beams were issuing from both your eyes. Do not blink.

According to every rule of concentration, no other thought should be permitted to enter your mind and all your attention must be focused on compelling the needle to change its position by about 45 to 90 degrees. Breathe slowly and rhythmically as this may accelerate the result. If your concentration has been strong enough, the needle will gradually start to turn as desired. Later on, the process may become much faster, as your experience grows and with it your will-power.

In many occult schools, especially those of Tibet, there is much importance attached to this exercise. However, as was stated earlier, we will forego the esoteric trimmings and get right to the heart of the matter. The exercise has its value as it is relatively easy to understand and perform and is a visible test of Para-X Powers.

If well performed, it may give the student much self-confidence and faith in his Para-X Powers, apart from incontestable proof of the possibility of influencing matter by the direct concentration of the human will, with all the resultant sequences, which the student can investigate and realize for himself.

TO CENTER YOUR THOUGHTS

"Concentration" is a word derived from two Latin words, i.e., "con," a prefix meaning "to;" and "centrum," meaning "center" or "fixed central point." The two words combined mean, literally, "to bring to a common point; to focus," etc. Thus the word "Concentration" is seen to mean, literally, "the act or state of bringing to a fixed point or focus."

Borrowing an analogous illustration from physical science, we readily see that the highest forms of energy, force or power are manifested by bringing the force to a focus, center, or common point thereby directing to that point the entire energy employed, instead of allowing it to become dissipated over a larger area. The electricity generated by a battery or dynamo, if allowed to diffuse itself over a large surface manifests but a small degree of the power that may be obtained from it by compelling it to discharge itself from a small point of focus. The same is true regarding the power of steam, which manifests great power by being forced to discharge itself through a small point or opening instead of being permitted to spread itself widely in the air. The same law applies to gunpowder, which manifests force by its gases being compelled to escape through the small gun-barrel instead of spreading in all directions, which it would do if unconfined.

Another familiar example is that of the magnifying glass, which brings the rays of the sun to a common point or focus, greatly intensifying the heat and light by reason thereof.

The Masters of Para-X Powers have ever impressed upon their pupils the importance and necessity of acquiring the power of Para-Concentration and all trained and developed occultists have practiced and persevered toward this end, the result being that some of them attained almost miraculous mental powers and influence. All occult phenomena are caused in this way, and all occult power depends upon it.

Therefore the student of Para-X Powers should devote a lot of thought, time and practice to this most important branch of the subject. It is a fact known to all students of Para-X Powers that very few persons possess more than a very small degree of concentration. They allow their mental forces to become scattered and dissipated in all directions, and obtain little or no results from the same. In the degree that a man is able to concentrate, so is he able to manifest mental power. A man's power of mental concentration is to a great extent his measure of greatness.

Para-Concentration, in practice, consists of focusing the mind upon a given subject, or object, firmly and fixedly, and then holding it there for a certain time, fully intent upon its object, and not allowing itself to be diverted or attracted from its object. It likewise consists in the correlative power of then detaching the mind from that subject, or object, and either allowing it to rest, or else focusing it upon another object. In other words, it either gives undivided attention or else inhibits (or "shuts off") attention from the given subject or object.

To the reader who has had no experience along the lines of Para-Concentration, it may seem like a very easy task to focus the mind upon a subject, and then hold it there firmly and fixedly. But a little practice will undeceive such a person and will bring him to a realizing sense of the difficulty of the task.

The mind is a very restless thing, and its tendency is to dance from one thing to another, darting here and there, soon tiring of continued attention, and like a spoiled child, seeking a new object upon which to exercise itself. On the other hand, many people allow their minds to concentrate (involuntarily) upon whatever may strike their fancy, and, forgetting everything else, they give themselves up to the object attracting their attention for the moment, often neglecting duties and important interests, and becoming daydreamers instead of firm thinkers. This involuntary concentration is a thing to be avoided, for it is the allowing of the attention to escape the control of the will. The Para-Concentration of the occultists is a very different thing, and is solely in control of the will, being applied when desirable and taken off or inhibited when desirable.

Those trained in Para-X Powers will concentrate upon a subject or object with a wonderful intensity, seemingly completely absorbed in the subject or object before him, and oblivious to all else in the world. And yet, the task accomplished or the given time expired, he will detach his mind from the object and will be perfectly fresh, watchful and wide-awake to the next matter before him. There is a difference in being controlled by involuntary attention, which is a species of self-hypnotizing, and the control of the attention, which is an evidence of mastery.

CONTROL OF ATTENTION

The secret of Para-Concentration lies in the control of the attention...and the control of the attention lies in the exercise of the will. All of the Para-X Masters begin teaching their pupils Attention as the first step toward Para-Concentration. They instruct the pupil to examine some familiar object, and endeavor to see as many details as possible in the object. Then after hearing the pupil's report, the master sends him back to the task, bidding him seek for new details, and so on until at last the pupil has discovered about all concerning the object that can be discovered. The next day a new object is given to him, and the process is repeated.

PARA-X POWERS

First simple objects are given, and then more complex ones, until at last objects of great complexity are easily mastered.

In this way not only is the power of close observation highly developed, but also the faculty of Attention becomes so highly strengthened that the pupil is able to exert the greatest amount of mental concentration with scarcely the consciousness of effort. And such a person then becomes a very giant in the manifestation of Para-X Power, for he is able to mold his mind "one-pointed," as the Masters describe it, until he has focused and directed a mighty degree of mental influence toward the desired object.

The person who uses Para-X Powers must certainly possess the power of focusing the force to a common point, in order to manifest the greatest amount of power and influence. And that faculty of focusing results from the training of the mind along the lines of concentration. And concentration arises from the mastery of voluntary attention. So there you have the whole matter in a nutshell. So your first step toward acquiring Para-X Powers should be to cultivate voluntary attention.

We might fill page after page with exercises designed to strengthen your faculty of voluntary attention, but what would be the use? The best plan is to set you to work to find something upon which to concentrate, for the very search will develop attention. Look around you for some object to study in detail. Then concentrate your attention upon it until you have seen all there is about it to be seen, and then take up another object and pursue the practice further. Take a page – this page, if you will, and count the number of words on it.

Then see how many words are required to fill each line, on an average; then see how many letters there are in each word, in each line, on the whole page. Then go over the page and see if any words are misspelled, or if any of the letters are imperfect, etc. In short, get acquainted with this page, until you know all about it. Then take up another page, and after studying it in the same way, compare the two and so on.

Of course this will be very boring and tedious unless you take an interest in it. And, remembering just what the exercise is designed for may arouse this interest. After practicing this way for a short time each day, you will begin to find that you are able to bestow greater attention upon objects upon which you are trying to manifest mental influence. You are developing Para-Concentration, and that is the great secret of the use of Para-X Powers, and explains the difference in its manifestation among men.

Now try this...close your eyes and rid your mind of all the clutter you have accumulated. Picture a peaceful scene in your mind. It might be a garden scene or it might be the ocean waves crashing on the sand. Now take yourself there. Picture yourself actually walking through that garden or along that beach. This might take a little while but with practice you will be able to go to your place immediately.

Once you get to your peaceful place it is time to proceed further. Think about your best friend. What is your friend doing right now? Is your friend at peace or is something bothering them? Try taking your concentration to a deeper level and see if you can get inside your friend's mind. Make a mental note to call your friend later and let them know what you found.

When you learn how to develop Para-X Powers you will eventually be able to see what is going on within a stranger's mind. Your friend was easier because you knew something about them but when you continue to strengthen your Para-X energy you will possess the ability to read the energy which surrounds anyone you meet.

ALLOW THE MIND TO REST

Another method of Para-Concentration is known as Calm Abiding, or allowing the mind to rest. In the Tibetan language, concentration practice is called shi-nay. The use of this word is based upon the recognition that our mind performs best when we are friends with ourselves, rather than looking at our mind as something evil or as an unruly child that needs harsh punishment in order to learn discipline. Forcing one's mind to concentrate may work for a while, but it binds up vital energy to maintain the level of tension that inevitably en-sues from such a struggle. The meaning of shi-nay explains the meaning of the practice, which is to teach the mind to remain at rest by leaving the thoughts and emotions that agitate and disturb it alone.

By learning to calmly abide with the object of concentration one can eventually maintain a focused state of mind indefinitely because it becomes a self perpetuating feed-back loop. A single pointed mind generates a relaxed, blissful feeling due to the gathering and strengthening of the body's vital energy. When our vital energy is strong we feel comfortable and invigorated. Pleasure naturally attracts the attention of the mind, like nectar attracts bees, making it easier (and more fun) to concentrate. Such one-pointed focus, if done properly, does not remove one from the every day world but brings it more into focus and releases tension from the mind so one is able to think and react more clearly.

Calm concentration is not done with a knit brow nor is it a narrowing down of one's awareness to exclude all other perceptions. That is a sort of tense concentration which most of us are familiar with in daily life. Calm concentration is effortless, natural and is not distracted by sensations or thoughts. In fact it includes all sensations, thoughts and feelings without partiality or compulsion. The quality of the mind at rest can vary greatly; it can be a coarser or finer state of mind. The coarsest state is a hibernation-like lethargy that is the opposite of calm abiding.

Calm abiding is a state in which mind is not in conflict with its thoughts; it is undisturbed and remains alert and lucid. If the mind lacks clarity, it goes into a state of dullness, torpor or sleep and calm abiding is lost. The mind should be neither too tense, because then it is agitated, nor too lax, because then there is the risk of falling asleep.11 Like a stringed instrument whose strings must be neither too tight nor too loose in order to play in tune, the mind should rest attentively.

After much patient training one can begin to dwell on the object with ease and grace. Experiences of contentment or the absence of thoughts often occur. When thoughts do occur they are less upsetting to the delicate balance of the mind poised between the agitation of distractions on one hand and a loss of awareness on the other.

Through proper training you can learn to fully engage in the world without losing the object of concentration. If you strain at holding onto an object then the mind will become only more wound up and tight with tension. One is then easily interrupted and characteristically such a person becomes irritated at perceived intrusions. It is important to begin training by developing an attitude of nonchalance toward interruptions.

If during a practice session you are interrupted, allow it to be okay, just relax and do not automatically get upset merely because someone dared to intrude. I am not saying that you should never be upset, that you should suppress your emotions, or not react appropriately to stimuli. What I am saying is to look at how your mind works when you happen to get interrupted during practice. Do you automatically become irritated with the intrusion? I believe there are people and spirits who can willfully try to interfere with magical rites. I encourage you to protect yourself in an appropriate manner from such beings before beginning any practice session or ritual if you feel the need. However, for purposes of training your mind to concentrate it is important to discover how your mind reacts to sudden change. Understanding this will help you develop a greater mental flexibility to move with daily changes without losing your balance.

Tibetans have for centuries developed a psychic technology in much the same way our culture has developed a material technology. In general, to learn the knack of abiding in a calm and focused state there are two main approaches: learning to fix the mind with a support and fixing the mind without a support. A support is any object, whether physical or imagined. Usually, mastery in fixing the attention upon an object is achieved first before you continue on to practice fixing your attention upon non-substantial infinite vastness, which is without thinking of the past, present or future, free from contrivance, fabrication or alteration of the natural mind. Learning to fix the mind without a support is an antidote to obsession and furthers the development of Para-X Powers by opening the mind beyond our everyday concerns.

Some techniques include both approaches together in order to facilitate a faster and more graceful development of concentration. Also, some methods of learning concentration use vocal sounds to integrate the various stages of learning. When one first starts to practice concentration one often notices that the mind acts like a waterfall: thoughts are constantly tumbling over one after another, each one pulling at us to follow, distracting us from the object of concentration.

After training a while, the mind becomes like a stream, with the thoughts flowing more slowly and steadily. One can start to perceive intuitive feelings arising in between the thoughts. After continued practice the mind becomes like a clear, serene lake with mysterious depths of feelings and insights. With more practice the mind is said to become limitless and unfathomable like the ocean, constantly in motion but never moving. This is a natural state of calm abiding in which focusing on anything for any length of time is effortless.

Such an experience may seem far-fetched to most Westerners. In general we are charged up mentally, swimming in a sea of changing emotions and thoughts, raising us up and dropping us down. How can we possibly live in a calm state without our minds filled with constantly churning thoughts? The method of fixing your attention upon a single object is one way to begin. Choose an object you feel good about, something you like or that has a special meaning to you. This is so you will feel happy when you practice, which will encourage you. The object can be something physical or totally imaginary. It is easier to imagine an object or symbol that you are already familiar with. It is not a good idea to use a bright, shining physical object because that would damage your sight.

Place the object in front of you, either physically or seeing it in your "mind's eye." If you have a tendency to lethargy or if you find that you are falling asleep during the practice of fixing your mind, then place the object up higher so that you fix with your eyes wide open. With an imaginary object, you can imagine that it is radiating brightly colored light to prevent torpor and increase the clarity of the object. If, however, you are agitated or easily distracted then place the object lower so that you are fixing with your eyes half closed.

If you are feeling neither sleepy nor distracted then place the object at a comfortable height. During a practice session it is common to shift between sleepiness and agitation, simply notice how you are doing and adjust the height of the object appropriately.

Once you have your chosen object in place and are sitting comfortably, start by fixing your mind sharply upon the object. Put all of your attention on it, using your mind like a sharp knife with all the aspects of your being pointing directly toward the object. As you fix sharply, you have no thoughts; they are automatically blocked. It is not beneficial to remain this way for long. If you do, then when you finish you may notice you are nervous. So, to start, only fix for a few seconds and then slowly relax the mind's focus. When you relax you will notice thoughts again arising to the surface of the mind. Observe the power of the thoughts and how they manifest in your mind until you become completely distracted from the object of concentration.

Once you notice that you are no longer dwelling on the chosen object, immediately fix your attention sharply on the object. Don't hold the sharp focus for long, again try to relax slowly and observe your mind. Continue on in this way during the entire session. Stop when you begin to become tired and start again only when refreshed.

By practicing in this way you can learn to integrate relaxation with concentration and thus stop fighting against yourself to achieve the ability to concentrate anytime, anywhere. Once you notice and discover the nature of the state of calm abiding, with practice you will be able to enter that state of mind. Abiding in an open frame of mind gradually frees our experience from the chain of compulsively conditioned thought. Directly experiencing our sensations without a commentator makes it easier to abide calmly in the world. This makes it possible for us to remain alert and relaxed while effectively engaged in any situation.

Developing our power to concentrate develops our will power and benefits us in developing our Para-X Powers. Without the ability to focus we are lost in a sea of whimsy or distracted too easily from our goals. Through the skill of concentration we can open any door to knowledge, wisdom or power and thus make Para-X Powers an immediate reality.

4
PARAPATHIC POWERS
READ THE THOUGHTS OF OTHERS

AT one time or another, nearly everyone has had the experience of being with someone when one of the two would make a remark and the other somewhat startled, would exclaim, "Why, that's just what I was going to say."

Nearly everyone has had experiences of knowing what a second person was going to say before the person spoke. As well, it is a very common experience to be thinking of someone a few moments before that person called on the phone or came knocking on the door. Many of us have suddenly found ourselves thinking of a person who we hadn't thought of in months, or even years, when all of a sudden that person would unexpectedly show up.

Mark Twain once wrote of a plan that he had frequently practiced, i.e., that of writing a letter to a person upon some subject, then addressing the envelope and inserting the letter, and then tearing the whole thing into pieces instead of sending it. He stated that in a large percentage of such cases he would receive within a short time a letter from the person to whom the destroyed letter had been addressed, answering the questions asked, or else speaking along the same lines as those of the destroyed letter. We have known of this experiment being tried on people thousands of miles away from the writer, and also in cases in which the other person had not been heard of for many years.

This amazing Para-X Power is known as Parapathic Power: the ability to read minds. Perhaps the best available evidence of Parapathic Powers is that found in the records of the English Society for Psychical Research. The experiments of the members of this Society and other investigators have resulted in the piling up of a mass of facts more than sufficient to fully establish the correctness of the theory of Parapathic Powers. Series of carefully managed experiments have been conducted, the results of which have conclusively proven that the thought-waves set into motion by the mind of one person may be consciously received by the mind of another.

THE CREERY EXPERIMENTS

One of the interesting series of experiments conducted by members of the English Society was that of the family of the Rev.

PARA-X POWERS

A.M. Creery, of Derbyshire. England. This investigation was made upon hearing the report of the Rev. Mr. Creery regarding a number of experiments he had conducted with his four children. He reported that he had begun by practicing a variation of what is generally known as the "willing game," in which one of the party leaves the room, and the company selects some object to be hidden, after which the person is recalled to the room when the company concentrates its mind upon the hidden object, and the seeker eventually finds it by means of Mind Reading. The reverend gentleman said in his report to the Society:

"We began by selecting the simplest objects in the room; then chose names of towns, people, dates, cards out of a pack, lines from different poems, etc., any thing or series of ideas that those present could keep before the mind steadily. The children seldom made a mistake. I have seen seventeen cards chosen by myself, named right in succession without any mistake. We soon found that a great deal depended upon the steadiness with which the ideas were kept before the minds of the thinkers, and upon the energy with which they willed the ideas to pass. I may say that this faculty is not confined to the members of one family; it is much more general than we imagine. To verify this conclusion I invited two of a neighbor's children to join us in our experiment, and very excellent results we secured from them."

The Society then began a series of careful investigations extending over a period of one year. The utmost care was taken to obviate the chance of fraud, collusion, mistakes, or outside influences. The experiments were conducted partly in Mr. Creery's house and partly in rooms selected by the members of the investigation committee. Having selected at random one of the children, the child would be taken from the room and accompanied by a member of the committee would wait out of sight or hearing of the room. The remainder of the committee would then select a card from the pack, or else write down a name or number which occurred to them at the moment. The following verbatim report of what followed will give you an idea of the results generally obtained. The report goes on to say:

"On re-entering the room the little girl would usually stand with her face to the wall, placed thus by us. But sometimes she would stand with her eyes directed toward the ground for a period of silence varying from a few seconds to a minute, till she called out to us some number, card or what it might be."

The report states that in the case of giving the names of objects chosen, the child scored six cases out of fourteen. In the case of naming of small objects held in the hands of members of the committee, she scored five out of six. In the case of naming cards she scored six out of thirteen. In the case of stating fictitious names chosen by the committee she scored, at a first trial, five out of ten.

One of the experiments is reported as follows:

"One of the children was sent into an adjoining room, the door of which was closed. The committee then thought of some object in the house and wrote the name down on paper. The strictest silence was observed. We then all silently thought of the name of the thing selected. In a few seconds the door of the adjoining room opened, and the child would appear generally with the object selected. No one was allowed to leave the room after the object had been fixed upon; no communication with the child was conceivable, as her place was often changed. Further, the only instructions given to the child were to fetch some object in the house that we would fix upon and would keep in mind to the exclusion of all other ideas. In this way we wrote down, among other things, a hairbrush it was brought; an orange it was brought; a wine-glass it was brought; an apple it was brought," etc., etc.

The report to the Society sums up the following results:

Three hundred and eighty-two trials were made in the series. In the test of naming the chosen letters of the alphabet, cards, and numbers of two figures, the chances against the girl were 21 to 1, 51 to 1, and 89 to 1, respectively. In the case of stating chosen surnames the odds against her were very much in excess of the figures just named. In the cases of the experiments of naming chosen cards it was calculated that a mere "guesser," according to the law of probability, would be able to correctly name but seven and one-third out of a total of the three hundred and eighty-two trials.

The actual results obtained by the child were as follows:

On the first attempt, one hundred and twenty-seven; on the second attempt, fifty-six additional, and on the third attempt, nineteen additional making a grand total of two hundred and two successes out of a possible three hundred and eighty-two! On one occasion five cards straight running were successfully named on a first trial. The mathematical chances of a mere "guess" doing this feat, under the Law of Average, or Probabilities, are estimated at over a million to one against the chance. And this was not merely an isolated, exceptional case, for there were other "long runs"; for instance, there were two cases in which runs of eight straight consecutive successes were scored once with names, and once with cards. In the case of the eight consecutive cards it ha been figured that the chances against the girl would figure up at least 140,000,000 to 1, according to the Law of Average and Probabilities. To understand just what this means it may help you if you will think

PARA-X POWERS

that the feat was like picking out one chosen man in a population of one hundred and forty millions, nearly double the population of the United States. And yet there are people who would dismiss matters like this with the remark, "mere coincidence."

The interest in the Creery children attracted the notice of Prof. Balfour Stewart, LL.D., and Fellow of the Royal Society. This distinguished gentleman testifies as follows:

"In the first instance, when I was present, the thought-reader was outside a door. The object or thing thought of was written on paper and silently handed to the company in the room. The thought reader was then called in, and in the course of perhaps a minute the answer was given. Definite objects in the room, for instance, were first thought of, and in the majority of cases the answers were correct. These numbers were thought of and the answers were generally right, but, of course, there were some cases of error. The names of towns were thought of, and a good many of these were right. Then fancy names were thought of. I was asked to think of certain fancy names and mark them down and hand them around to the company. I then thought of, and wrote on paper, 'Bluebeard,' 'Tom Thumb,' 'Cinderella,' and the answers were all correct."

Subsequent experiments with the Creery children, at the house of the well known investigator, Mr. F.W.H. Myers, at Cambridge, England, proved equally successful. The children, and their ages, were as follows: Mary, 17; Alice, 15; Maud, 13.

The percentage of successes obtained at Mr. Myers house tallied very well with those obtained elsewhere. One remarkable result was obtained, though, that had not been obtained before. On one occasion the child was asked to name the "suit" of cards chosen one after another. That is, of course, the child was asked to name which suit, "hearts," "diamonds," "clubs," or "spades," were shown of the card drawn and seen by the committee, and then thought of. On this occasion the child scored a run of fourteen straight running, consecutive successes. The chances against this success were 4,782,969 to 1.

MAN USES PARAPATHIC POWERS TO FIND WALLET

Another interesting case that happened in 2005 involved Tom Meade of Phoenix, Arizona. Tom was out one Saturday when he realized that he had lost his wallet. He had been to several different places that day but had not used his wallet in any of them.

Tom, using his Parapathic Powers, cleared his mind and allowed his thoughts to roam free. Immediately he got the impression of a woman wearing a blue sundress picking his wallet up off of the floor and rummaging through its contents. He quickly sent a Parapathic message to this woman that she MUST immediately contact him by any means possible.

At that moment, Tom's cell phone rang, someone had found his wallet. When Tom went back to the store to pick it up, the finder was a woman wearing a blue sundress. She told him that she felt compelled to call Tom herself, rather than simply turning the wallet in to the store owner.

By using his Parapathic Powers, Tom was able to read and send an impression to the mind of the woman. This is equally amazing due to the fact that Tom had never met this woman before, yet through Para-X Powers, was able to tune in to her mind and find his lost wallet. Not only is it possible to read minds from a distance using Parapathic Powers, it is possible to implant your own thoughts into others so that they MUST do your bidding.

We could go on and on relating various cases and experiments proving the existence of Parapathic Powers. But there is a way that is far more convincing than reading about experiments that were conducted years ago, and that way is to learn for yourself how to unleash your own Parapathic Powers. It only takes a little practice and soon you will not only be able to read minds, but you will also be able project your thoughts into the minds of others.

TWO TYPES OF PARAPATHIC POWERS

Parapathic Power is divided into two types: "Contact" and "Telepathic." The first of these types, "Contact" Parapathic Power, is demonstrated by physical contact between the Transmitter (or active agent) and the Receiver (or passive agent) in order to afford an easy channel for the passage of the vibrations, thought-waves, nerve-currents, or magnetism of the Transmitter. The second class, "Telepathic," is demonstrated by the transferal of the "waves," "vibrations," "energies," or "magnetism" of the Transmitter to the Receiver through space (often for thousands of miles) without the more convenient "wires" of the nerves of the two agents.

There is a striking analogy between electric phenomena and mental force phenomena all the way through the subject, and this subject of Parapathic Power is simply one of the many forms of the resemblance.

We shall begin by giving you instructions in Contact Parapathic Power, as it is the simplest and easiest to accomplish. And besides, the best mind readers have been trained by means of

PARA-X POWERS

the practice of Contact Parapathic Power at the start. After one learns how to use Contact Parapathic Power, the next step is to learn how to accomplish mind to mind Parapathic Power.

Anyone may develop himself, or herself, into a good Contact mind reader by practice, and perseverance. As in everything else in life, some will succeed better than others; and some will find the work easier than do others, but all may develop quite a respectable degree of proficiency in a short time. A little careful, conscientious practice and experiment will accomplish wonders.

Parapathic Power depends upon the will and concentration on the part of the Transmitter, and upon the degree of receptivity and passivity of the Receiver. You should start out by practicing privately with the help of a few, good friends. By careful and repeated practice you will gain confidence by your growing success in your experiments.

Begin your exercises by selecting one or more friends who are in sympathy with you, and who are interested in the subject. Do not have any unsympathetic or uncongenial persons around you when you are practicing, for such people tend to distract your attention from your work, and really exert a detrimental effect upon the preliminary work. Select one of your friends as the Transmitter and take the part of the Receiver yourself.

Begin your practice by establishing a psychic harmony, or rapport, between yourself and your Transmitter by means of rhythmic breathing. Although this feature of the work has been overlooked by many investigators of the subject, still it is a very important feature of the work, and one that is conducive to the production of the very best results along these lines of psychic demonstrations.

When two persons are in "rapport" with each other, there is a mental and psychic harmony between them, which is productive of the best possible mental cooperative work. Hence the necessity of good rapport conditions with Parapathic Powers.

Rhythmic breathing has been known to occultists of all ages as one of the important adjuncts of psychic phenomena. Rhythmic breathing consists in the person breathing in slow measured regular rhythm. It may be acquired by counting the indrawn breath, the retained breath, and the outgoing breath, by regular beats like the ticking of a large clock. For instance, draw in your breath slowly, counting mentally according to the ticking of an imaginary large clock: "one two three four." Then hold the breath, counting "one two." Then breathe out slowly: "one two three four."

The rule is that the indrawn breath should have the same number of counts as the outgoing breath. The principal point about rhythmic breathing is that the two persons, the Transmitter and the

Receiver, should breathe in unison with each other that is in perfect time and rhythm. This breathing in unison will soon establish the very best psychic harmony conditions between them. From four to seven rhythmic breaths will be enough to establish the proper conditions in ordinary cases.

Begin all practicing with rapport breathing. You will find that it has a very soothing, calming, quieting effect upon both persons, and will produce in each a mental earnestness and concentration that will help along the demonstration of Parapathic Powers.

A CLEAR IDEA

You should begin your session by establishing a clear idea in your mind. The main idea is that the Transmitter be able to concentrate his will upon the mind of the receiver, impressing upon him the sense of direction so strongly that he will move in accordance with the Will of the Transmitter.

Begin by blindfolding yourself and have the Transmitter stand beside you in the center of the room. Have him mentally select a corner of the room, saying nothing to you of his choice. Then let him concentrate his mind upon that one corner, forgetting every other part of the room. Then have the Transmitter grasp your left hand with his right hand, you grasping his fingers in your hand and lifting the hand to your forehead.

Hold the hand against your forehead, just above your eyes. Instruct him then to will that you go to the corner of the room that he has selected, shutting out all other thoughts from his mind, and concentrating his entire attention upon the projection of his will. He must not content himself in merely forming a mental picture of the selected corner, but must think of the direction of that corner, just as he would in case he were to wish to walk there himself. He must not simply think "That Corner" he must think "There!" using the sense of direction. He must will that you shall go there, carrying the words "Go There!" in his mind.

You, the Receiver, must place yourself in a perfectly passive and receptive state of mind, resigning your own will for the time being, and being perfectly willing and desirous of being mentally directed or led by the will of the Transmitter. He is the active factor, and you the passive. It is the strength of his will, and the degree of your receptivity that makes the demonstration a success. Keep your eyes closed, even though you are blindfolded, for by so doing you induce a passive state of mind, and even the stray glimpses that you may catch through the handkerchief will serve only to distract you. You must shut out sights, and even thoughts of sights.

Stand quietly a moment or two, awaiting impressions from the mind of the Transmitter, who is making the mental command: "Go there; go there." while at the same time he is willing that you follow his command.

After a moment or two of passive and receptive waiting, you will begin to feel an impulse to move forward. Obey this impulse and take the first step, which will often be in an opposite direction from the selected corner. The idea of this first step is to "get started." While you are taking the first step or two, you will feel a clearer impulse toward the real selected corner, and will find yourself swinging around to it.

Don't become impatient, for you are but learning to receive the impressions. Advance one foot forward and you will soon feel yourself being compelled to move in a certain direction, which will end in your moving toward the correct corner. You will soon become conscious of being directed by the will of the Projector, whose mind is acting upon yours and leading and directing you toward the right place.

It is difficult to describe to you the exact feeling that you will experience, but a little practice will soon make it clear to you. Follow the impulse, and you will soon begin to feel the mental command, "This way this way, no, not that way but this way," until you reach the desired spot, when you will feel the command: "That's right stop where you are this is the place."

If you start to wander off in the wrong direction you will begin to feel the correcting impression: "This way, this way," and if you will but passively receive and follow the mental telegraph message you will find the impulse growing stronger and stronger until you walk right into the corner selected.

When you walk in the right direction, you will feel the mental message, "Right, right"; and when you move in the wrong direction you will feel the mental message, saying, "No, no, not that way!" By practice, you will soon become more sensitive to these guiding thought-waves, and will act upon them almost automatically.

Practice will soon so sharpen your perceptive faculties that you will often be able to move right off to the desired corner at once, sometimes actually running right to it, dragging the Transmitter after you. Practice this exercise and experiment, in different rooms, and with different Transmitters, until you can go readily to the selected corner.

Do not be discouraged, but remember that "practice makes perfect," and that like any other thing the art must be learned by patient practice and repetition.

PARA-X POWERS

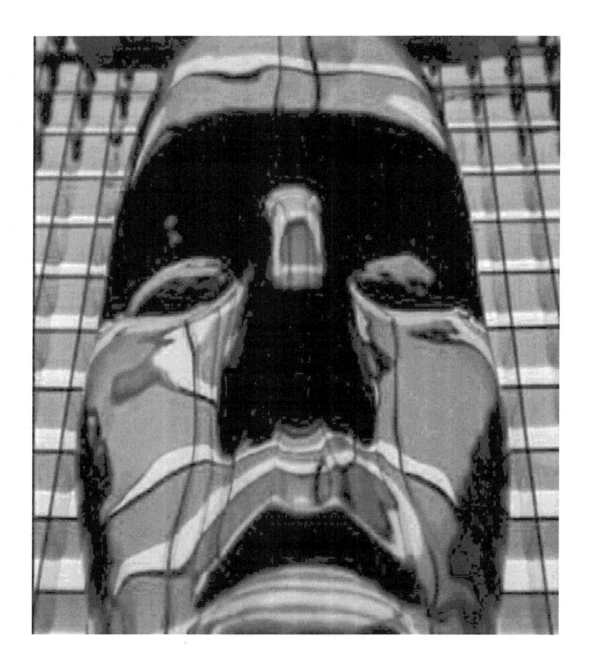

Everyone has the ability to read the minds of others. All humans emit electromagnetic energies at frequencies that are receivable by other human minds. With a little practice, the natural filters that block such mind-to-mind contact can be pushed aside with amazing results.

PARA-X POWERS

It is like learning to play the guitar, skating, dancing, or anything else. If after a number of trials you begin to feel tired, stop practicing until the next day. Do not strain yourself, or wear out your mind. When the next day comes you will be surprised at the added proficiency you have gained.

After you have grown capable in locating the corners of rooms, you can have the Transmitter select other parts of the room, such as doors, mantels, windows, alcoves, projections, etc. Try a number of these selected locations in turn, gaining a variety of experiences which will prove valuable later on. In all of these experiments the transmitter must guard you from running in to obstacles, furniture, etc., by telling you to avoid them, guiding you past them, and in other proper ways prevent you from bruising yourself or upsetting things. Don't allow your mind to be distracted by outside things.

FINDING LARGE OBJECTS

The next step should be the selecting and finding of large objects in the room, such as chairs, tables, etc. Proceed as in the previous exercises. Do not neglect this exercise in your desire to do more wonderful things, for you need just this training. You will realize the importance of these exercises after you begin to appear before friends and evening companies, etc., when you will be called upon to find hidden objects, selected articles secreted under tables, on persons, on furniture, etc.

If you can find selected chairs you will be able to more readily find persons seated on chairs. Continue this exercise until you can readily find any and every piece of furniture in a room and the other large objects in a room as well, when they are thought of by the Transmitter. After mastering the above exercise have the Transmitter select some small articles, such as a book, vase, ornament, etc., on a table, mantelpiece, etc. Proceed as before, varying the objects and places, endeavoring to get as wide a range of experiences as possible.

FINDING HIDDEN ARTICLES

After you have mastered the last mentioned exercise, have the Transmitter select a small object, such as a watch, key, match, etc., and hide it in some part of the room. Proceed as before, until you find the hidden object. Have him place a key in a book, under a rug, back of a picture, and in similar difficult places. Let him

43

exercise his ingenuity in finding strange places in which to hide the object.

In the experiments in finding the hidden objects he must train himself to give you the mental messages "up"; "down"; "to the right"; "to the left," etc., just as he did his old message or impulse "this way." And you must train yourself to receive them. This training will be of the greatest possible benefit to you when you are called upon later to find objects hidden in people's pockets, etc.

The above exercises will train you to receive and act upon the mental commands or messages of the Transmitter, under a great variety of circumstances and conditions. In finding a hidden object, the first thing to do is to get an idea of the direction. Then the general location of the hiding place; and so on, from general impressions to detailed ones, until at last the fingers close upon the object itself. Thus the Transmitter will be greatly relieved when the object is finally found, and the relaxing of his mental tension may be distinctly felt, and then you will know that your search is at an end.

MIND TO MIND CONTACT

After you have gotten comfortable with Contact Parapathic Powers, now is the time to learn mind to mind contact. Start out much as the same with Contact Parapathic Powers, have a friend hold a certain number of small buttons, etc., in his hand, and try to will that you "guess" the right number. A similar experiment with the pack of cards, the student endeavoring to "guess" the card drawn from the pack, naming color, suit, and number in turn, may afford successful results. Remember that the "guess" is not a guess at all, but an attempt to register the mental impression of the Transmitter.

Your mind should be held as receptive as possible, that is, "open" to vibrations. Take your time, and do not let hurry or anxiety enter your mind. It will be well to practice this experiment with members of your family, or with harmonious and sympathetic friends.

Experiments of Parapathic Powers may be practiced between friends at long distances, space apparently presenting no obstacle to the passage of the thought waves. Pick out some friend with whom you have established a strong rapport by means of his having acted as your Transmitter in your Contact experiments, and by having practiced rhythmic breathing.

Have the transmitter sit in his room at the appointed time, gazing intently at some small simple object, such as a knife, a glass, a cup, a book, etc., and endeavoring to make a clear mental picture of it, which picture he should also Will to be reproduced in your mind. Remember he should think of the looks or appearance of the object not merely of its name. He should think of the shape, etc., of the book, instead of thinking the word "book." At the same time you should sit quietly in your room, placing yourself in the same passive, receptive mental attitude that you have acquired and practiced in your Contact experiments. Then wait patiently for impressions. After a while, if successful, you should get the mental picture of a book, or whatever object was thought of by the Transmitter.

Another way of conducting experiments along the lines of the Parapathic Powers is akin to Automatic Writing. The Transmitter concentrates his thought and Will in the usual manner, while the Receiver places himself in the usual receptive, passive state of mind, and awaits the impressions. But instead of the Receiver merely sitting as usual, he draws his chair to a table, having pen in his hand and a pad of paper on the table before him. He holds the pen lightly between his fingers, with its point touching the paper and then awaits the impressions.

Under good conditions, after waiting a time, the pen will begin to twitch and move feebly. The hands and fingers should allow it full and free motion. After a few moments of indecision the pen will often begin to write out words. In many experiments the word or object thought of by the Transmitter will be written out, or drawn in full by the hand of the Receiver acting automatically. Some experimenters succeed much better with this plan than with the more common method. If you are not used to writing with a pen, try sitting in front of your keyboard and letting your fingers type out the mental impressions that are flowing through you.

RECEPTION OF THOUGHT

Now you may proceed to the actual reception of thought from another mind, with no physical contact. Thought will pass directly from this person's mind into your own. To begin with, observe these rules: 1. Remember that a calm, not-too-anxious mind functions best. Use deep relaxation for this purpose. Do not clench your fists or grind your teeth. Relax, completely and deeply; make your mind a blank, ready to receive any impression. 2. Enlist the aid of a friend or friends who are likewise relaxed and patient. It would be advantageous if these are the friends with whom you practiced Contact experiments. Now I shall give you some powerful secrets of

PARA-X POWERS

Mind Reading. Use them and you will succeed beyond your wildest dreams.

First of all, as a general rule, when reading the mind of a good friend, try to think of all the qualities which he or she possesses. If you are standing face to face with the person, look at this person intently, from time to time, without making him feel uncomfortable. Try to get the feel of this person's personality, how he walks, talks and moves, his likes and dislikes, his temperament, how he reacts to different situations, what he's likely to be thinking about at this moment. Finally, when you are completely "attuned" to this person, relax, and you will find to your amazement that the thoughts come.

To test the accuracy of the thoughts you receive, simply repeat them and your friend will exclaim: "That's right! That's exactly what I was thinking! Why, you must be a mind reader!"

Even a beginner can get such results. Secondly, when attempting to read anyone's mind, always wait for those times when he or she seems most relaxed and "at ease with the world." If the person is smiling or humming to himself, that is a good time to start mind reading. If you happen to be speaking to this person and be seems contented or in a good mood, that, too, is a good time to read his thoughts. Similarly, you will find that the thoughts of others come to you with greatest clarity at those times when both you and the other person are in a good mood. If possible, try to avoid reading the mind of someone who is troubled or upset, until your Parapathic Power has strengthened considerably from great use.

PARAPATHIC POWER AT A DISTANCE

There are also some tricks you can use when practicing long distance telepathy with a friend. If you are a beginner (assuming you want things as easy as possible), plan to practice in the early morning, late afternoon, or at night. The atmosphere around you is clearest at these times, free of radio waves that might interfere, as well as sunspot ions. You should especially practice receiving at dawn or earlier, since everyone's mind, including your own, is most relaxed at that time.

To practice, have your friend send you a brief message at this time (he may even be in another city). The message should be brief, but ask your friend to concentrate on it for at least a half-hour, without letup, willing that you will understand what it is. A good idea would be for your friend to have the message written out (printed) and to concentrate on it.

PARA-X POWERS

In order to tune in on this person, however, it will be necessary, in the beginning, to have a good idea of his or her physical surroundings. If possible, visit the place where he will be, and show this person your surroundings. Exchange photographs of the rooms you will use. Memorize these pictures. Tell your friend to trace the two points between your homes with his finger on a map, and you do likewise. This process is somewhat like directing an antenna onto the right beam. Indeed, physiologists picture the brain as having near its outer surface billions of tiny nerve ends aimed as if they were aerials for directional radio.

At the appointed hour, you should be holding in your hand, or elsewhere against bare skin, some bit of material which has been in close contact with the other party. (In the Polynesian Islands, those who wish to send or receive a telepathic message often try to obtain clippings of the person's hair or fingernails.) Such a personal antenna constitutes an actual link between minds across space, since all objects and creatures emit energies that vibrate at the same rate as the object from which they arise. When you hold such an object, belonging to another person, against your body, you become more strongly attuned to his energies, or vibrations.

WE ARE ALL CONNECTED

Scientists have discovered that if a photograph is taken of an object, the digital image will be saturated with the same radiations as the object, and will continue to give off these radiations for some time afterwards. More startling still, these radiations seem to constitute an invisible channel between the object and the photograph, linking the two. When the vibrations of various foods, such as water and minerals, are reproduced in an oscillator and beamed at the photograph, the plant is nourished without food.

This secret, called "psychometry," may be used also in sending messages, since it helps constitute an actual telephone link between two people. But for now we are concerned with receiving other people's thoughts.

For your experiments, any small objects will do, such as ring, a pin, an earring, or some trinket, a watch, a hairpin, keys, a pen or pencil, a glove, tie or handkerchief, anything will do as long as it has been in frequent or prolonged contact with the owner's body, or is an object at which he gazes frequently (such as some bauble or knick-knack on a desk). Try to select objects belonging to your friend which have not been touched by anyone else.

PARA-X POWERS

While awaiting your friend's message, hold your hand against the object that belongs to him, or press your finger or palm against it. An object such as a watch, or a bracelet that fits snugly, may be fastened to your wrist. (It would be helpful if you don't mind revealing this secret, if he were doing the same with an object belonging to you.) This will link your two personalities, by means of their radiation frequencies, across time and space.

If at any time, you should have trouble, ask yourself, "Am I trying too hard?" And if you are, try to forget the object of this experiment and relax. Do not practice receiving while lying down or tired, lest you drowse. If you feel you may be tired at the appointed time, allow yourself a few minutes beforehand to have a cup of coffee or an energy drink. (Research has shown that the caffeine present in coffee and energy drinks often helps in telepathic communication.)

Keep your eyes closed most of the time, and put yourself in a relaxed and passive attitude. (In the course of your experiments, it would be helpful, if you experiment with various objects.)

USE YOUR INNER-EAR

Here is another powerful secret which you may use if you wish to read your friend's mind at a distance, the Para-Phone. This will help draw his thoughts to you. The main principle of this technique is that it helps your "inner ear" concentrate by removing all outside distractions.

There are several ways to do this, ranging from a simple use of your hand to an actual earphone (such as the kind used with MP3 players). The first of these methods requires complete silence and involves the use of your hand. Cup your hand to your ear, resting the edge or base of your palm against your cheek or jaw. Keep your thumb away from you. Best your fingers above your ear, against the side of your head. Arch the body of your hand so that it never touches your ear.

Tilt your head slightly in the direction in which you are listening. Now think of the person whose mind you are trying to read. Picture him as situated wherever he is likely to be. Try to get the "feel" of this person's personality, as mentioned before: how he walks and talks, his likes and dislikes, his temperament, how he reacts to different situations, what he's likely to be thinking about at this moment.

The purpose of your hand is to increase the flow of electricity to your brain. As was stated earlier, your body is filled with electricity, which may be channeled to and from the body, or to any part of the body desired. Electricity, for example, is created by the friction of your blood running through arteries and veins. The electricity so generated can be channeled, through your fingers, to enter whatever is touched.

By concentrating on your friend's voice, for example, a thought current is set up in your brain. It is of exactly the same wave length and frequency as the thought in your friend's mind.

By placing your hand to your ear, near the auditory nerve, you sensitize and increase the power of your "inner ear" to "hear" this wave frequency, which is then translated into the actual thoughts of the person whose mind you are reading.

The thought currents emanating from your friend's mind, wherever he is, might be compared to the ripple set off by a pebble thrown into water, making larger and larger circles.

That is what radio waves look like, and it is no more remarkable that you should be able to pick up your friend's thought waves, out of thousand of others, than it is for your radio to pick u one station out of thousands and thousands that are sending radio signals into the atmosphere.

More important than anything I could say describing this technique is the simple fact that it works. But it requires concentration, the concentration of your "inner mind."

Another way to achieve such concentration is to "lull" your outer ear into a sort of slumber or light trance, walling out outside noises and distractions. This enables the inner ear to concentrate and attune itself to the thoughts of the person whose mind you wish to read. (The trance, by the way, can be broken at any time, simply by shifting your eyes or moving your body in some way.)

To do this, the outer ear is deliberately fixed on, or fascinated by some steady sound or beat, such as the sound of boiling water, steam, or a running faucet. This is called "white noise."

Any hollow object that you can hold to your ear will do, such as a seashell, a paper cup, an ordinary drinking glass, teacup, or round, bowl-shaped ashtray. A piece of hollow rubber tubing would be excellent. A somewhat fainter sound may be obtained by holding one or both hands to your ears.

As you can see, no wires, batteries, or motors are necessary. To produce the steady "hollow" sound, the object should have some indentations (such as an ashtray or a seashell), and be held lightly to the ear. The end of a tube that is open at both ends should be held as firmly as possible to the ear.

If you wish, you may use a more sophisticated instrument that produces white noise. A radio tuned between stations, a television that is not on a broadcasting channel. There are even some

Internet sites that have recordings of white noise for various psychic purposes.

When you find yourself comfortably concentrating on this sound, you will be able to shift your "inner mind" to the contemplation of your friend, as described before. His or her thoughts should soon come to you with unmistakable clarity.

OVERHEAR CONVERSATIONS WITH PARA-PHONE

In his book, *Enigmas of Psychical Research*, James Hyslop reports the following experience of a beginner with the Para-Phone: "Miss G. F. had been experimenting with a friend for telepathy. Some time after he had left, she picked up her shell and held it to her ear. The conversation which they had had at the experiments was repeated in an aural hallucination, and in the midst of it came the words: 'Are you a vegetarian then?' Miss G. F. at once wrote to her friend, stating the facts, and asked him if he was responsible for this (fragmentary message). He replied that about fifteen minutes after he had left her he met a friend who made some allusions to a vegetarian restaurant, and that he, Miss G. F.'s friend, had interrupted him with the question: 'Are you a vegetarian, then?'"

THE AMAZING POWER YOU NOW POSSESS

When you have followed the steps outlined for you in this chapter, you will be in a position of great advantage over others. With the Para-Phone, for example, you will find that you can actually hear the unspoken thoughts of any person who happens to be standing near you, and that you can even tune in on these people at a distance of many miles, if you so choose.

You may find yourself standing next to someone in the supermarket, for example, looking at his silent, smiling face and hear him thinking about what a fine day it is, how he would like to go bowling, or any number of things. At first, you may catch just a word, or several words. But as your Parapathic Power develops, you will find that you can easily "read" complete thoughts.

Used wisely, this power can aid you enormously. Ever wonder, for example, when making an important purchase, such as a house, a car, or a computer, whether you were being cheated, overcharged, or stuck with a lemon? Parapathic Power can be your insurance against being taken advantage of.

The Para-Phone has helped countless people find and marry their perfect mates. Women find it a help in judging their boy friends (and the opposite is also true). In one instance, the Para-Phone revealed the culprits in an office plot to the man who was being victimized by their scheming. In another case, the Para-Phone revealed the exact location of a child who was locked in a department store after closing time by accident, and who was pleading for help.

Your Parapathic Power can reveal business plans and opportunities long before they are announced. Many a low-paid worker has risen to wealth simply by "tuning in" on the minds of his bosses and superiors with Para-X Power.

You can double your salary and get rapid promotions with practically no effort at all, simply by tuning in on your bosses' minds. Finding out what needed to be done, as well as how to do it, long before anything was mentioned. In this manner, will seem that you are smarter and harder working than those around you.

HOW TO MAKE MORE MONEY

In these tough economic times, every little bit can help you get ahead. Real estate and car salesmen have doubled, tripled and quadrupled their salaries, and in some instances, have even become partners with their bosses, or have eventually taken over the business all because of their knowledge of Para-X Powers.

There are many small shopkeepers, for example, who, by using this power to "tune in" on the minds of customers, have been able to stock up on fast-moving products and quickly sell them at a huge profit. By being able to read people's minds, they have been able to find out what they like to talk about, what moods they are in, so that these people come back time after time and bring their friends, simply because they like these shopkeepers, who always seem to know how to please them. As a result, what was once a small, hole-in-the-wall, shoestring operation, rapidly blossomed into a large, thriving business. All it takes is a little practice and the willingness to open your mind to new ideas and thought patterns.

Even more amazing, it is possible for anyone, using Parapathic Powers to "tune in" on the Mass Mind (the minds of thousands of people at once), through relaxation, visualization, and concentration exercises, to discover gold-mine opportunities: single, small desires such as a way of saving time or money when shopping, a desire for a new fad which is rising up in people's minds (like buying up gold and silver, or a book series that is going to become popular with teen-age girls), and many other desires which, if shared by enough people, need only be offered to them by you to make you a fortune.

PARA-X POWERS

To tap the Mass Mind for such information, all you need do is follow the procedures for concentration and visualization exercises given in this book, willing beforehand that your mind will be attuned to the general desires of the mass of humanity around you. The strongest impressions you receive, those that arise time and again during your sessions, are the ones that will be the news of tomorrow. Money-making ideas that you can cash in on now by planning your strategy, by finding a way to provide the product or service cheaply, by stocking up on an item (if it is already in existence) now, while you may still do so cheaply before there is a run on the market for it.

MAKE MONEY WITHOUT WORKING

Fortunes have been made on the stock market with this technique. You might discover a business that was soon going to be in big demand, then all you do is buy stock in that company while the price is low. I know a man who regularly makes thousands of dollars a week this way, without lifting a finger. Another man built a retirement fund of $500,000 in just a few years. And still another, a man in his sixties, who made $10,000 in three months, using this technique.

Yet every one of these people, and many more, including housewives, retirees and others who have made money by leaps and bounds with Para-X Power, swears that he does not know a single thing about "high finance."

But that's the least of it. For by tapping the Mass Mind, as shown in this chapter, the entire plan for a fabulous new money-making idea may be laid out before you. A striking example of this is the early automobile. Did Henry Ford actually conceive of the notion of a cheap, horseless carriage and a way to mass produce it all by himself? Or did he, in fact, simply tap the Mass Mind through Para-X Power? Many think he did, for at the time several prominent inventors were working on the same idea in strictest secrecy.

HOW THE PARA-PHONE CAN HELP
WITH PERSONAL PROBLEMS

What else can Parapathic Power do for you? Last but not least, it can help you in your personal life. For example, say you have a troubled friend or neighbor: by reading his mind, you will know the nature of his problems and be able to exercise sympathy

PARA-X POWERS

and understanding. What might otherwise have appeared to be rudeness or thoughtlessness on this person's part, you will then understand to be deep thought. You will understand why, perhaps, he forgot to say good morning, was curt or gruff with you, and you will not be offended.

The Para-Phone can also help you understand a wife, a husband, a son or daughter better. Teenagers, especially, will benefit by your understanding at a time in their lives when they are apt to feel lonely and confused and have a hard time expressing themselves openly. It can help you mend a troubled marriage, strengthen and unite all family ties.

With the passage of time, your Parapathic Power will cease to be a novelty and become a very handy tool that you can use to good advantage, one that you can "turn on or off" at will.

But in order to keep this power, it is necessary to use it. Keep practicing, every chance you get: at the supermarket, the gas station, at work, or dining lunchtime. Use it without shame, for it is a God-given power that was meant to help us, not hurt us, to help us live more easily. And it is a power that money cannot buy, simply because you already possess it.

5
HOW TO SEDUCE OTHERS WITH PARA-X POWERS

This chapter explains the little-known method for seducing another person using Para-X Power. Providing you follow the steps clearly and patiently, these techniques will open you up to a hidden world around you and give you a peek at just how easily you can influence others.

This ability must be used with great caution and discretion. Even though this ability can lead to a lot of pleasant and even profitable ventures, it can also lead to a lot of pain and suffering to all involved. Remember, just because you can use this power on others, doesn't mean that you should. You should always use wisdom with the use of this power.

As human adults, we are already well versed in the experience of mind manifestation. When you look around you in your everyday life, you will see countless examples of a human's ability to manifest "stuff" from thought.

All manmade things first began in the thoughts of a person, or a group of people. Imagination plays a key role. The idea/concept is first birthed in the mind. Then the idea is discussed, either with oneself or with others. There is more mental work done to paint a final manifested picture in the mind(s). Finally, the idea is taken into aspects of physical processes which start the manifestation process, bringing the original mind-birthed idea into full manifestation in the physical world.

Even how you arrange your furniture is an example of thought-to-manifestation, whereby your plans/ideas are first created in the mind then you do the physical process (like moving your furniture around the room) to completely manifest your intended redecorating idea (thought).

Looking at the physical things around you are not examples of obvious or redundant things. They are all examples of mind/thought manifestation. When you begin to view your mental abilities in this light, you will begin to realize that you are well advanced in mind power already. On a subconscious level, your mind is a highly advanced machine: Just to name a few...it stores information, processes data, allows you to communicate with your spoken language, and also maintains regulation of all your bodily functions (advanced systems in themselves) without your conscious mind needing to do the work.

Keep these things in mind when you begin to enter the world of Para-X Power, for really, you are not a beginner at all. Your mind is truly amazing and you can already create physical things stemming from a single thought (idea). It is your inner attitude (belief) which offers that magic substance which will eventually open you up to even higher levels of Para-X Power and mind manifestation.

WHAT IS PARA-SEDUCTION?

The Para-Seduction of others' is the ability to erotically or sexually arouse another person using only the silent powers Para-X. When you apply these techniques on someone, that person will feel deeply attracted and sexually drawn to you. Most often, a condition of "falling in love" begins to take place upon the person you want to seduce. No communication with the person is needed. It need not even be someone you know. However, eventual communication will happen and should happen for it will provide you with valuable feedback as to the effectiveness of your Para-Seduction.

The methods presented here are without a doubt, very powerful. The effect begins instantly, however there will be a certain degree of lag time before you physically see results. Instant and automatic sexual influence is a mental skill that takes time. Like any skill, you need to develop it through effective and regular practice. You must maintain patience and calm rather than trying to hurry the process up.

As your skill increases, manifestation will come quicker. If you are new to these techniques, then expect anywhere from a couple of weeks to a few months for results to be seen. Results are directly influenced by the amount of time you involve yourself in this, at least during these beginner stages. Patience and calm pays off though, for you will begin to see your influence taking effect and molding into manifestation on a physical level; that person will become so drawn to you that eventually they will want to be with you.

LET'S GET STARTED

Let's start out by calling the person you would like to seduce your "target." Your target is your goal, your intention. To reach your intention, you must first decide upon which individual you want to influence. Most people have their eye on someone already; someone whom they want to be with.

You need not have had prior or current communications with your target. They can be someone with whom you have never spoken. It is preferable though, especially during these "beginner" stages, that it is someone you see frequently, like someone you work with. Later, as you progress in this art, you do not even have to be in the same city as your target.

For now, find someone close to you, someone you will see often, so you can glean feedback. Being able to observe the person during the period you are influencing them offers you valuable feedback. Feedback is a tool which not only helps you progress with your skill at mind power influence, but it can steer you in the right direction when you are working on a target project.

Remember, you are not only using your mind to manipulate thought and feelings of another person, but also to manipulate events and circumstances; all this for the final goal to eventually manifest your initial intent. Monitoring your target (gaining feedback) allows you to better assess a situation or follow the progress of a series of events. With careful observation and planning, you can learn to best gear your influence in the most appropriate way or frequency of practice.

Once you have found your target, you should keep a notebook or something akin to that to keep track of all your observations. Keeping notes is a valuable tool which will increase your overall Para-X Power influence skill level.

THE PARA-X INFLUENCE

When you begin to use Para-Seduction to influence another person, a vast array of things will happen. Some of these things are observable (and should be recorded) and some not so apparent. People react in different ways to Para-Seduction influence. Some submit easily, others with resistance. But all of the reactions point to one inevitable occurrence: The target will become very, very drawn and attracted to you. The feelings will be deep and strong, and resemble "falling in love" emotions.

At no point will the person feel like they being forced or influenced. Even if the feelings might feel strong (which is common) or confusing (which is rare), the target will only feel like it is themselves that are starting to be drawn to you. Then the target will eventually reach out to start communicating with you more.

It is advisable to not flirt in anyway at first with the person you want to influence. Just focus on being friendly and funny (making the other person smile/happy) and allow your seduction influence to do its work. Often a target will put up walls of sorts if they know that someone is just trying to hit on them. Act friend-like only, while your influences are making them more drawn to you.

PARA-X POWERS

Don't jump the gun if you get a good sign that they now have erotic feelings towards you. Be patient and allow the conscious mind of the person to feel good towards you. All the while you are programming their subconscious mind with your intent.

YOUR DAILY ROUTINE

The first thing you need to do is set up a daily routine. These are the techniques which you will be putting into gear towards your goal of Para-Seduction.

First, find one hour a day. The hour is split in two Para-Seduction sessions: Thus you will be doing a half hour session at one time in a day, and another session at a later time in the same day. If need be, reduce each session by 15 minutes, but it is preferable to do half hour sessions. Serious Para-Seduction adventurers may even find the desire to do longer sessions, perhaps two or more hours a day. Keeping notes of your sessions is also advisable.

The process of mental seduction is done through specific visualization methods. Your thoughts have an uncanny ability to manipulate your surroundings; effectuating change within the physical world. If you are seeing something within your mind's eye (via imagination, visualization, etc.), providing it is done in a patient, confident, and repetitive manner...it will begin to manipulate the ether around you and have pronounced effect upon the events and people in your life.

CALMING THE MIND

It is crucial that your session begins with a calming of your mind. In other words, you need to be in a comfortable relaxed state to do your sessions. As your mind relaxes, your electrical brainwave patterns lower in their frequency. These brainwaves then become more in sync with the natural frequency pulse of the planet (7.85 cycles per second) and thus facilitate a resonance between your mind and the physical world around you. Relaxing the mind also enables you to visualize easier and your bodily functions are kept to a minimum.

We have discussed in previous chapters how to relax and calm the mind, just follow those techniques and allow a comfortable relaxed state to occur and your visualizations will still be effective. Over time, you can train yourself to go into deeper states of relaxation.

PARA-X POWERS

Too often, beginners worry or focus on issues such as just how relaxed to be, or whether or not their visualizations are clear. The most important thing to remember is that practice brings skill, and this will develop over time. One should not worry or obsess over issues of mental clarity or precise relaxation methods, but rather one should focus more on doing the actual seduction visualization techniques on a frequent basis, allowing the skill level to improve naturally over time.

Without this frame of thinking, one can easily spend more time worrying about technicalities or theory data, rather than actually working with the specific visualization methods. Too often, people embarking on a spiritual quest tend to get lost in the vast array of information out there and spend less time on actual personal application of the spiritual teachings they are investigating.

You can spend years reading the books and arming yourself with facts, theory, and information. Then you find out you do not spend much time doing personal experimentation and action. This is why so few actually attain a high level of personal power, although they may have every book on the subject. So when relaxing your mind and beginning your sessions, don't worry if you are relaxed enough or if you are doing the methods properly...just do the work and the skill and technicalities will improve and become refined over time.

INFLUENCING YOUR TARGET

Your half hour session should include the following two forms of visualization. 20 minutes should be used to erotically "touch" (in your mind) the other person. The last 10 minutes should involve "scenario building." Let's go into more details.

For the sake of simplification, visualization can be viewed simply as imagining, as if daydreaming. Simply allow yourself to imagine. Whether or not you can see things clearly in your imagination is not important. Visualization clarity develops over time through practice.

For the first twenty minutes you need to imagine yourself touching the target in a sexual/erotic way. Focus more on the touch itself and the effect that the touch is having on the other person, not on the situation or scene that you are in. Keep your touches gentle and erotic, not rushed or aggressive. In your mind's eye (imagination) focus more on the feeling of touch, rather than seeing yourself touching.

For some practice on feeling (touching) things in your mind, imagine yourself touching cotton balls, or touching a pen, or touching some rocks. Take your time and caress these objects in your mind, feeling the hardness or softness, etc. But these practice sessions are separate from your seduction sessions.

Erotically caressing someone involves some knowledge or experience in sexual intimacy. If you have had some prior sexual experiences, then you already can come up with ways to erotically touch someone. If you have no experience prior, then just use your imagination as best as you can.

Erotic touches and caresses should be focused on typical erogenous areas of the target's body, such as the nipples and genital areas as well as other tender areas of the body such as the neck or face. As you touch that person in your mind, feel (as best as possible) the reaction the other person should experience, such as wetness (if the target is a woman) or hardness (if the target is a man). You want to slowly erotically touch the person and feel their reaction building in your mind, eventually driving them to a sexual frenzy. Take your time and don't try to rush over the touches, trying to cover all sensual parts of their body. Different areas can be explored in different sessions. Once again, the target's "turned on" feeling as a result of your mental touches should be prominent in these visualizations.

The final 10 minutes of your half hour session should be visualizing you and your target together in scenarios. If you are trying to instill a feeling of "falling in love" within your target, then imagine (visualize) you and your target hanging out, holding hands, cuddling on the couch, etc. If you want a strictly sexual relationship, visualize you and your target having intense sexual encounters in exciting locations and situations. Imagine how you and your target feel the excitement, tension and intense fulfillment when you finally come together in pleasure.

Find one thing to focus on and keep that scenario for the entire 10 minutes. In these scenario sub-sessions, try to encompass as much emotion and senses as possible. You can see the target, touch the target, hear their voice, see the surroundings of where you are, etc.

Most important to visualized scenarios is the feeling of "now." You want to experience the scene in your imagination as if it was happening in the present moment. Not later, not then...but NOW.

To add that extra dosage of belief into the process, when you are doing your session you should hold yourself with an inner smile...an inner knowing that your efforts are working and have come to fruition. Even if you feel doubtful, fake the feeling. It will eventually become your feeling. The feeling is that confident holding of oneself with that unbreakable faith that your Para-X Power is highly effective and powerful.

PARA-X POWERS

With that inner confident feeling, you also instill patience, seriousness, and calm...which are all emotions (energy) which work in conjunction with your visualization sessions (thoughts) to eventually manipulate and change the physical world around you (e.g. making events happen).

This describes the half hour session you must do. 20 minutes of mentally and erotically touching someone, and their deep arousal/reaction to it. Then 10 minutes of situation scenarios. This total session should be done twice a day preferably. Be patient and have faith, and don't be in a rush to see results immediately. Even if an outward response takes a couple of weeks, you are not wasting any time whatsoever by doing the daily sessions. On the contrary, you are training yourself in new mental efforts, you are training yourself to have patience (which means confidence that things WILL manifest as you are commanding), and you are continually charging up the influences upon the other person.

YOUR INFLUENCE

Your influences are having an effect upon your target. The visualizations (thought commands) are seeping deeply into your target's subconscious mind. And they are starting to have erotic or loving feelings towards you. In most cases, the target usually tries to not show these feelings...just like you are not revealing all your emotions as you carry on your daily life around others. But in time you will see signs.

Your target is beginning to think about you. And soon they will begin to have erotic feelings towards you. They will find themselves becoming more and more drawn to you. When they are alone, they may find the need to fantasize about you, especially after you have done numerous days of sessions upon them. They will probably occasionally dream about you as well, while they sleep.

During this time, purposeful monitoring of the other person's reactions is vital. In your notebook, keep careful notes of their behavior around you not matter how trivial it may seem. Even if you are not in communication with the target, you can merely observe them when you see them.

If you talk or know the target, then monitor signs when you are talking to them. And remember what was mentioned above. If you are communication with the target, just offer yourself to them in a friendly and enjoyable (perhaps funny) manner...not in a flirty way. If the other person senses that you are trying to flirt with them...then emotional walls on their part may go up. This is an annoying wall to break down with your Para-X Power.

Taking an interest in the target, asking questions about them, this is another great way to break down walls. Just act as if you are a safe and fun friend or acquaintance, and you provide a clear path for effective thought transmission.

As you start to get feedback from the person, you can study the trend of the behavior; watch how it grows and weans, or goes up and down, or obvious to discreet. Don't feel silly to write down in your notebook, "Target made eye contact with me, and looked at me with a smile."

Monitoring feedback also offers another way of helping to mold events to your favor. For example, if you start to sense that the person is becoming friendlier to you...you can initiate more interaction with them.

Be faithful with the methods, and keep notes of your efforts and your target's reactions. That person is now erotically driven to be with you. Without doubt, it will happen.

PRACTICE, PRACTICE, PRACTICE

Always be confident in your powers and enjoy the process of learning to advance these skills. Experimentation is vital but don't go way off into your own methods until you have gained repetitive results with the methods presented here.

Keep up with your practice. If you do daily sessions, a year from now your skill will be of a surely higher level. Never give up on a target. Even if you choose a new target, you can still work on the previous one at the same time (extra sessions). Be sure and think about the ethics of the issue prior to venturing off into mind control methods.

If your intentions are positive and not harmful, then you will be fine. If you wish to use your powers to hurt or be violent to others, then you are the proud winner of a collection of negative forces which will seek to guide you down a darker wider path.

Don't tell the person you are trying to influence them, for obvious reasons. Don't tell anyone you are using methods on someone else (others' doubt can add resistance to your efforts). By using your Para-Seduction Powers, you can soon learn how to influence and manifest the events you want. As time goes by, you will learn to develop methods on your own, based on experimentation and practice.

PARA-X POWERS

Remember, the one who develops the skill with Para-Seduction, is the one who is master at controlling others and master at preventing being controlled by others.

ATTRACT A NEW LOVER WITH PARA-X POWERS

Para-X Power can be used as a one-way telepathic communication. According to Caitlin MacKenna, it can be directed to a particular person, or it can be broadcast like a radio or television signal. One use for Para-X Power is to attract a new lover with particular qualities that you want, or to attract a particular person. Using Para-Seduction to attract a new lover is a simple process. You don't have to believe in it; you just have to do it.

First, start by creating a thought form of your ideal lover, or of the particular person whom you are trying to attract. Close your eyes and imagine the body of your lover life sized in three dimensions. Take as much time as you need to do this step. The more vivid your mental image, the more effective your mental influence will be.

Second, in your mind, begin making love with your lover thought form. Be as realistic as you can. Involve all of your senses. You must feel the thought form body when you touch it.

Third, while making love with your lover thought form, think about his or her qualities. Say to yourself, "I love your hair color, eye color, the softness of your skin, etc. Continue with this type of inner dialogue during the lovemaking. Picture the qualities of your lover as vapor inside his or her body.

Fourth, when you feel ready, transfer your Para-X energy to your lover thought form. Picture your energy in the form of a vapor flowing from your penis or vagina and filling the thought form.

Fifth, you can repeat step 3 and 4 as long as you want though spending 15-30 minutes on your Para-Seduction influence session is about right. When you are finished, don't think about it anymore. If you keep thinking about your objective, your thought form stays attached to you. You have to release your thought form, so it can reach its target.

The sixth step requires that you repeat the steps 1-5 daily until you achieve results, which could take from a few hours to a few weeks. If you don't get results within a month, there are three possible problems: 1. your mental imagery is not vivid enough to create a viable thought form; 2. you are obsessing about your objective, and, thereby, not allowing your thought form to reach its target; or 3. you are not getting out or going anywhere that you could meet your new lover.

PARA-X POWERS

Some say that using Para-Seduction to attract a particular person is wrong because it "violates free will." Magical traditions all over the world disagree with that viewpoint, and I personally don't see how mental influence is different from the other methods people use to attract new lovers, such as sexy clothes, perfume or cologne, music, etc. However, if you do think that it is wrong, don't do it. Just use Para-Seduction techniques to attract your ideal lover, leaving it to the universe to send the right person.

When using Para-Seduction techniques, some people meet with resistance from their target. Signs of resistance show you that your Para-Seduction is starting to work. It does not mean that your efforts will not work. All it means is that it will take longer for the programming to be successful.

OVERCOME RESISTANCE

Caitlin MacKenna has also pointed out that when using Para-Seduction techniques, some people meet with resistance from their target. Your prospective lover may be cold, rude, or even hostile towards you. Though it may be hard to believe, that's a good thing, not a bad thing.

Signs of resistance show you that your mental influence is starting to work. It does not mean that your efforts will not work. All it means is that it will take longer for the programming to be successful.

Here are five ways to overcome resistance to Para-Seduction.

1. You can apply longer and more intense visualizing until the person's resistance breaks down. This will increase your influence even if the person is suppressing their feelings or ignoring you. They will learn that resisting you will cause more visualizing on your part (of course, this is all on an subconscious level since they don't consciously know that you are using mental influence techniques on them.)

2. You can make a U-turn and visualize them very much attracted to you while, at the same time in your visualizing, you give them the cold shoulder. When you visualize, make them want you and be very eager to please you while you brush them off and reject them. This can break the person's resistance completely because their mind cannot understand this influence or how to resist it, and, therefore, the person is defenseless. As well, nothing attracts a person more than thinking that they can't have you.

3. You can stop doing your Para-Seduction sessions for a few days and then start again with more force. Continue this stopping and starting if the person still resists. These pauses can be very effective because, when you are holding off on your techniques for a few days, the subconscious mind of the person feels that the pressure is off, and the person begins to let down their defenses. When the defenses go down, all your visualizing begins to creep into the person's mind. When your mental images are blocked, they don't fade away. They just "hang around" until an opening is found into the person's mind. If the person is resisting, the visualizing you have done just waits and accumulates until there is a clear opening into the mind (such as when their defenses are down).

4. If the person is showing signs of being fearful about the new sexual feelings you are creating in them, use your visualizing to slow down the passion. It's sometimes best to begin with a gentle approach, and then later you can slowly build up to intense, erotic scenarios. Visualize being friends at first and doing friend-type things (non-threatening) and then work up to sexual things after a few weeks. This technique is especially important if you are trying to get a person to fall in love with you. You first visualize the person being happy and comfortable with you; maybe laughing and playing, and then put in the sexual scenarios when you have fully instilled the "safe" scenarios.

5. If their unconscious mind can't handle the load of your influence, the person may even try getting away from you. This can occur even if they don't know you, but are resisting subconsciously. It doesn't matter how far the distance (the farther the better) since their defenses will go down. You can continue to do your work, and your influence will gain entry into their mind much more easily. If you continue your mental influence after they move, they will begin to miss you terribly. The only problem is that you won't be able to monitor their reactions or signs of changed behavior, but that's no problem because sparks should fly the next time they see you.

If the person you are working is resisting to some extent, then work with one or all of these techniques. Be very alert of their signs so that you can use the best technique. Some people get ill from energy/strength loss when trying to wrestle against your influence. Sooner or later, their subconscious mind will give up if you keep up the work. With Para-Seduction, they will become yours.

PARA-X POWERS

Para-Seduction is not hypnotism...you do not force anyone to do anything against their will. Instead, by using Para-X Power, you are able to achieve mind-to-mind contact at the subconscious level to initiate romantic or sexual interest within the mind of your target.

6
PARA-INFLUENCE: HAVE OTHERS OBEY
YOUR SILENT COMMANDS

WILLIAM W. Atkinson was one of the first masters of Para-X Powers. It was from the diligent research of Atkinson that many of the Para-X techniques were first discovered. One amazing Para-X Technique as conceived by Atkinson is known as Para-Influence: using your mental energies to get others to do your bidding.

Mental-Induction: In physical science the term Induction is used to indicate that quality in a manifestation of energy which tends to reproduce in a second object the vibrations manifesting in the first object, without direct contact between the two bodies. Send the Thought-Waves forth charged with a great intensity of desire or will which will persist for a long time.

Mental Concentration: Mental Concentration, in practice, consists of focusing the mind upon a given subject, or object, firmly and fixedly, and then holding it there for a certain time, fully intent upon its object, and not allowing itself to be diverted or attracted from its object. It likewise consists in the correlative power of then detaching the mind from that subject, or object, and either allowing it to rest, or else focusing it upon another object.

Become a firm thinker instead of a daydreamer. The involuntary concentration is a thing to be avoided, for it is the allowing of the attention to escape the control of the will. The secret of Mental Concentration lies in the control of the Attention. And the control of the Attention lies in the exercise of the Will. The person who uses Para-Influence must certainly possess the power of focusing the force to a common point, in order to manifest the greatest amount of power and influence. Concentration is the great secret of the use of Para-Influence.

Mental Imaging: What is known as a "Mental Image" in occultism is the mental creation, in the imagination of a "picture" of the things, events or conditions that one desires to be manifested or materialized in actual effect.

You know that the clearer a Mental Picture you possess of anything that you want – the better you know just what you want – and the better you know the latter, the better able you are to take steps to get it. Do not allow your imagination to "run away with you" – do not become a dreamer of dreams and a doer of nothing. You must master your imagination and make it your servant and not your master. The feeling, desire or mental state sought to be transferred from one mind to others.

PARA-X POWERS

Fascination: By Fascination we mean the manifestation of Mental Influence when the two persons are together, without passes or the usual hypnotic methods. The fundamental idea is the forming of the thought, and then sending it out to the other person.

For instance, if you wish a person to like you, you should form in your mind this thought: "That person likes me," fixing it in your own mind as a fact. Then project to him the concentrated thought, "You like me – you like me very much," with an air of assurance and confidence, and the other person is bound to feel the effect unless he or she has acquired a knowledge of the subject and is using self-protection. The thought should be sent forth with the strength that usually accompanies a strong spoken statement, but you must not actually "speak" the words aloud – you should merely say them strongly in your mind. You are able to overcome his Will – using the silent message of "I am Stronger than you – my Will overcomes yours," etc.

The principle consists of: 1. The Thought of what the person wishes the other to do held firmly in the mind; and 2. The projection of that Thought to the other, silently, in the shape of unspoken words.

One person may fascinate another without understanding a word of his language, the real strength coming from the strength of the desire behind the words. The formation of the desire-thought into words is merely for the purpose of concentrating and focusing the thought, for words are concentrated symbols of ideas, thoughts or feelings. It may help you to imagine that you can see the force flying from you to the other.

The imagination properly used helps very much in these matters, for it creates a mental path over which the force may travel. You must not act awkwardly when sending out the Para-X energies, but converse in an ordinary manner, sending your Para-X energies between your speeches, when the other person is talking to you, or at any pause in the conversation. It is always well to send first a powerful Para-X energy before the conversation is opened, preferably while you are approaching the person.

Hypnotism: By Hypnotism we mean the use of the power, also, when the two parties are together, but accompanied by passes, eye-influence or hypnotic methods.

The two classes of manifestation, Fascination and Hypnotism, really blend into each other, and it is difficult to draw a dividing line in some cases.

Begin by having the person stand before you. Then make sweeping passes in front of the person from head to foot. Then make a few passes in front of the face of the subject, then along his arms. Then take hold of his hands and hold them a little while, looking him straight in the eyes. Make all passes downward. Avoid joking or laughter and maintain a serious, earnest expression and frame of mind.

Then standing in front of the subject tell him to take his will off of his legs and stand perfectly passive and relaxed. Then looking him straight in the eyes, say to him: "Now, I am going to draw you forward toward me by my mental power – you will feel yourself falling forward toward me – don't resist but let yourself come toward me – I will catch you, don't be afraid – now come – come – come – now you're coming, that's right," etc.

You will find that he will begin to sway toward you and in a moment or two will fall forward in your arms. It is unnecessary to say that you should concentrate your mind steadily upon the idea of his falling forward, using your will firmly to that effect. It will help matters if you hold your hands on each side of his head, but just in front of him, not touching him, however, and then draw away your hands, toward yourself, saying at the same time: "Come now – come – you're coming," etc. Standing behind the subject and drawing him backward may reverse this experiment.

Be sure and catch him in your arms when he falls to protect him from a fall to the floor. In the same manner you may fasten his hands together, telling him that he cannot draw them apart. Or you may start him revolving his hands, and then giving him orders that he cannot stop them. Or you may draw him all around the room after you, following your finger that you have pointed at his nose. Or you may make him experience a feeling of heat and pain by touching your finger to his hand and telling him that it is hot. All of the familiar simple experiments may be performed successfully upon a large percentage of persons, in this way, by following the above general directions. In the above experiments, be sure you "take off" the influence afterward, by making upward passes, and willing that the influence pass off. Do not neglect this.

A WORD OF WARNING

And now a word of warning – Beware of people who are always putting their hands on you, or patting or stroking you, or wishing to hold your hands a long time. Many persons do this from force of habit, and innocently, but others do so with the intention of producing a mild form of hypnotic influence upon you.

If you meet such persons, and find them attempting anything of this sort, you can counteract their influence by sending them a strong thought current, sending them the thought: "You can't affect me – I am too strong for you – you can't play your tricks on me."

PARA-X POWERS

It is a good plan to practice this counteracting force when you are shaking hands with a "magnetic" person who seems to affect people. You will soon be able to distinguish these people by a certain force about them and a peculiar expression in their eyes, at the same time using your protective will upon them.

PARA-INFLUENCE AT A DISTANCE

It is the manifestation of the influence when the persons affected are removed in space from the person using the influence. The principles underlying Para-Influence at a distance are precisely the same as those underlying the use of influence when the persons are in the presence of each other. The difference between present influence and distant influence is merely a matter of degree; the advantages accruing from the exception mentioned may be duplicated by practice and development in the case of distant influence.

One of the most elementary, and yet one of the most effective methods known to occultists is that of creating a Mental Image of the person "treated" in the sense of imagining him to be seated in a chair in front of the person treating him at a distance. The treater proceeds to give both verbal commands, and at the same time directs Thought-Waves, or Para-Energies, by talking mentally, toward the imaginary person seated before him. This process establishes a psychic condition between the treater and the actual person, although the latter may be removed from the treater by many miles of space.

In the above forms of treatment the treater treats the Mental Image, picture, etc., precisely as he would if the person were actually present. He forgets for the time being that the person may be hundreds of miles away, and concentrates his influence on the image, or picture, etc. In short, he acts as if the person were sitting before him, wide-awake, and receptive to his influence.

Another way, employed by some, is to begin darting Thought-Waves toward the other person, forming in the imagination a gradual lengthening "psychic-wire" composed of thought-vibrations. Those practicing this technique say that when the psychic-wire is projected sufficiently far (and it travels with incredible speed) and comes in contact with the mind of the other person, the treater feels at once that contact has been established, by a peculiar faint electric shock. Then the treater proceeds to send his thought-currents along the psychic-wire in the same manner as if the person were actually in his presence.

PARA-X POWERS

Another form of distant treatment consists in forming a Para-Tube. The Para-Tube is set up in a similar manner to the psychic-wire, and projected toward the person desired to influence. It is formed in the imagination as a smoke-ring, or a worm-hole in time and space. Visualize this ring to be about six inches to one foot wide. With your imagination, see this worm-hole lengthen out in the shape of a tube which rapidly extends and travels toward the person treated, in a manner identical with that of the psychic-wire.

Those following this method of distant influencing report that they recognize the completion of the tube by a sensation of stoppage and a feeling of "rapport" having been established between themselves and the other person. In some cases they report that they are able to faintly "see" the figure of the other person in miniature at the other end of the Para-Tube.

There are two other methods frequently used in distant influencing which we shall now briefly describe: The first of these two methods consists in sitting or standing in a quiet place, or rather in some place in which you can concentrate and then directing your Thought-Waves toward the other person, forming in the imagination a mental picture of the force flying from you toward the other, like tiny sparks of electricity. This mental picture tends to give a concentrative force to the current which renders them powerful, and sends them direct to the desired spot.

The second of these two methods is that used by the most advanced occultists who have advanced beyond the use of the methods described just now. These people simply stand or sit quietly and concentrate their minds until they attain the state of Mental Calm known to many as "the Silence." Then they create a strong mental picture of the person treated, surrounded by the conditions desired created, or doing the things desired to be done. This is one of the highest forms of Para-X Power and really approaches a higher phase of influence than that of the mental plane as generally known.

A picture of a person held in the mind in this way – the person being seen in perfect, robust health, and happy and successful – tends to materialize the same conditions in the person in real life.

DIRECT YOUR WILL TO INFLUENCE A CROWD

The most common form of Para-Influencing En Masse is the lesser degree manifestation, along unconscious lines manifested by a majority of people by reason of their desire for the success of certain things. By desire we do not mean the mere "wanting" or "wishing" state of mind, but rather than eager longing, craving, demanding mental state that evinces a hungry reaching out for the desired thing.

The constant dwelling upon some special object of subject, by men who have developed concentration, strong wills and fixity of purpose has the effect of sending out great circles of ever-widening Para-X Power, which sweep ever outward like waves in a pond caused by dropping in a stone.

Other appeals to the minds of these people will be far more likely to reach them than otherwise, for "interest" is the first step toward attention, and attention is another step toward action. And in the same way a person possessed of a strong fear of a thing will send out similar attracting waves, which have a tendency to attract or draw to him the people calculated to bring about the materialization of the thing feared. The secret lies in the fact that in both the case of Desire and Fear the mind forms the Mental Image, which tends to become materialized.

Occultists "treat" the public en masse by holding the strong mental picture of that which they desire, and then sending out strong thought-currents of desire in all directions, willing that those coming within their radius shall be attracted toward the ideas expressed in the Mental Image projected in all directions. Some masters of this art of influencing the public create a mental picture of themselves sending out great volumes of Thought-Waves for a time, and then afterward mentally imparting a rotary motion to the waves, until at last they form a mental whirlpool rushing round and round and always sucking in toward the center.

You will see from what has been said that an individual who has cultivated the faculty of concentration and has acquired the art of creating sharp, clear, strong mental images, and who when engaged in an undertaking will so charge his mind with the idea of success, will be bound to become an attracting center.

Daydreamers do not materialize thought – they merely dissipate energy. The man who converts thought in activity and material being, throws energy into the task and puts forth his will-power through the picture on the slide.

USE PARA-X POWERS FOR SELF-PROTECTION

It is true that we, and other writers on the subject of Para-X Powers, have shown that one is far less liable to influence if he maintainS a mental atmosphere of high vibration – that is keeping oneself surrounded by a thought atmosphere filled with vibrations of the highest kind of thoughts and free from thoughts and desire of a base, selfish character, which tends to attract similar thoughts.

The fact is that within each of us, in the very center of the being of each individual – in the very heart of hearts of the Immortal Ego – is what occultists know as the Flame of the Spirit. This is what you recognize in consciousness as the "I AM" consciousness – that consciousness of being which is far above the consciousness of personality, or the things of personality.

It is that consciousness which informs each individual, unmistakably, that he is actually an Individual Being. This consciousness comes to the individual by reason of his contact with the great One Life of the Universe – it is the point of contact between the PART and the ALL. And in this part of a man's consciousness, coupled with the sense of BEING an "I," there resides a spark from the Divine Flame of Life and Power, which is what has been called the WILL of man.

Now, do not mistake us and confuse this with the so- called Will of personality, which is merely a Desire, or else a certain firmness, which often is little more than stubbornness. This inner Will is Real Power, and when once recognized may be drawn upon as a source of unending and unfailing Strength.

When you come in contact with people who are seeking to influence you, you will find yourself able to defy their mental attacks by simply remembering the strength imminent in your "I," aided by the statement (made silently to yourself): "I am an Immortal Spirit, using the Will within my Ego." With this Mental Attitude you may make the slightest mental effort in the direction of throwing out from your mind vibrations, which will scatter the adverse influences in all directions, and which, if persisted in, will cause the other person to become confused and anxious to let you alone.

With this consciousness held in mind, your mental command to another, "Let me alone – I cast off your influence by the power of my Spirit," will act so strongly that you will be able to actually see the effect at once. If the other person is stubborn and determined to influence you by words of suggestion, coaxing, threatening, or similar methods, look him or her straight in the eyes, saying mentally "I defy you – my inner power casts off your influence."

Try this the next time that anyone attempts to influence you either verbally or by Thought–Waves and see how strong and positive you will feel, and how the efforts of the other person will fail. Above all, put out of your mind all fear of others persons. The feeling of fear prevents you from manifesting the power within you to its full extent.

PARA-X POWERS

Cast out fear as unworthy and hurtful. Not only in the case of personal influence in the actual presence of the other person may be defeated in this way, but the same method will act equally as well in the matter of repelling the mental influence of others directed against you in the form of "absent treatments," etc.

If you feel yourself inclining toward doing something which in your heart you feel that is not to your best interests, judged from a true standpoint, you may know that, consciously or unconsciously, someone is seeking to influence you in this way. Then smile to yourself and make the statements mentioned above, or some similar one, and holding the power of the Spirit within your "I" firmly in you mind, send out a mental command just as you would in the case of the actual presence of the person himself or herself.

You may also deny the influencing power out of existence by asserting mentally: "I DENY your power to influence me – you have no such power over me – I am resting on my knowledge of Spirit and its Will within me – I deny your power out of existence."

This form of denial may be used either in the case of absent influence or personal influence. The rule is the same in all cases.

7
PARA-COMMANDS TO BRING MONEY
AND GOOD FORTUNE

THE one thing that draws most people to a book like *Para-X Powers* is the desire to have more money (finding love and romance follows at a close second place). Bookstores are filled with all manner of books promising the reader the secrets of financial success. Online, there are thousands of websites, many also selling ebooks, that offer plans to make thousands of dollars a week without ever leaving the comforts of your home. The general consensus is that the majority of these books and websites do little to make money for anyone except the producers of the websites and books.

However, a close examination of some of the books and web pages show that they do offer instructions on helping people realize that they have the power to make their dreams and desires come true. As we have said throughout this book, our state of mind is crucial to how our lives work out. If you always have a bad attitude and expect the worst to happen, well, guess what? The worst usually will happen to you. On the other hand, if you go through life happy and optimistic, then usually good things come to you.

Of course having a happy attitude about life is not going to keep you perpetually free of heartache and sorrow; as it has been said: "In every life some rain must fall." No one is going to be completely free of bad things happening to them. For without the bad stuff, how can we appreciate the good stuff?

When you have a positive outlook on life it makes the bad stuff feel less bad. Your positive attitude allows you to shake off any negative feelings and lets you go on with your life knowing that tomorrow will be a better day.

This is how we are able to utilize the amazing energies of Para-X Powers. Our thoughts are just as real as this book you are holding in your hand. With the help of Para-X Powers, our thoughts become a physical reality. On the other hand, Para-X Powers can also make your negative thoughts a reality.

Negative thoughts are just as powerful as positive thoughts. Para-X Power cannot differentiate between the two. That is where your conscious mind comes into play. You are the creator of your reality. You make your hopes and dreams come true with Para-X Powers.

By striving to overcome negative thoughts and emotions, you allow Para-X Powers to work in your favor with your positive thoughts and emotions. If you feel bad, take a close look at your emotions and be honest with yourself on why you feel bad.

Rather than dwelling on these bad thoughts, think about what you can do to make yourself feel better. Focus on the good things in your life. Remember past feelings of happiness and excitement...a visit to a favorite amusement park; Christmas morning; sitting on your Grandmothers lap; drinking hot chocolate and eating cookies after playing outside in the snow.

These happy, excited feelings are how you should strive to feel every day of your life. You need to look at every moment of your life with that same sense of exhilaration that you had as a child on Christmas morning.

SALESMAN USES POSITIVE THOUGHTS TO WIN OVER CUSTOMERS

A car salesman that I know was having a bad time trying to meet his monthly quota selling cars. Times are tough right now and people are just not buying cars like they used to. Every day this salesman was becoming more and more depressed. It seemed that the more morose his outlook, the worst his days became. It had reached a point where it looked like he was going to lose his job.

Then he discovered Para-X Powers and realized that his negative thoughts and emotions were assisting in creating his negative reality. He made the positive choice that he was going to put a stop to his negative thoughts and work on recognizing his positive thoughts.

It was not easy for him to change the pessimistic thought-patterns that had become ingrained into his everyday existence. But slowly, day by day, he worked on finding the good things in his life and learned to truly appreciate them.

Positive thoughts breed more positive thoughts. It becomes easier, more natural to look at life with a sense of wonderment and excitement as if everyday were a totally new and unexpected gift. Positive thoughts naturally outweigh the negative.

Where once it was a daily grind, the car salesman now became eager to go to work. He started using his Para-X Power to send out positive Thought-Waves, Para-Commanding those thinking about buying a car to come and seek him out.

Slowly, but surely, people began to respond to his Para-Influence. The dealership saw a steady increase in overall sales. And the number one salesman was our good friend who only weeks before had been certain that he was going to be fired.

PARA-X POWERS

Not only did the salesman use positive thinking to change his reality, but he also brought Para-X Powers into play. Using positive Para-Influence, he inserted into the thoughts of others the idea to come to the car dealership; the need to find him and the desire to buy a car from him.

It may seem too simple to be true...that positive thinking can bring such a change to a person's life. But this is where people are fooled...it is this easy, it is this simple. You only have to have the desire, the will, and the patience to try it out for yourself.

CAUTION IN CALLING FOR MONEY

We have all heard the old saying: "Money does not grow on trees." Well this is true in both the physical and the astral worlds. You cannot wish money into existence. It always has to come from someplace.

What this means is that when using Para-X Powers to call for money, the Universe will generally find the path of least resistance to make your desire come true. This path of least resistance may bring your money from an unfortunate or even tragic situation.

One woman used Para-X Powers to command money, but did not provide a logical source for this money. Unfortunately, the money did arrive, when her husband died in a car accident and his life insurance policy paid out. So always be clear what you want when commanding the arrival of money.

PARA-CHANT TO BRING MONEY

The famous author of the esoteric, Raymond Buckland, in his book *The Power of Magic Chants*, provides a special chant for generating large sums of money. This chant provides the all-important energy for Para-X Powers to make this desire a reality.

Start this by spending at least an hour beforehand thinking positive thoughts about how nice it will be to have some extra cash. Think about how excited you will feel when this money arrives. Think about how happy you will feel knowing that this money came to you through happiness, and not sad or tragic circumstances.

Sit for a moment and think hard about the exact amount of money you need. See the money; see yourself holding it, counting it. Imagine not that it will come, but that it has come—that you now have it.

With this in mind, you may start the chant.

76

PARA-X POWERS

Try to think of the words, of what to say, as you chant them. Get the rhythm so that it is automatic. Sit, stand or kneel, whichever is more comfortable. Now say the chant out loud:

Suddenly I see the pile,

Suddenly I hold the sum,

Suddenly I end the trial,

For the money –it has come!

For the money — that I need.

For the need that is so strong.

For these words that I do read,

Brings the money right along.

Brings the money without waiting.

Brings the money right to me.

Brings the answer to my waiting.

Suddenly I will be free.

Look into your open hands and visualize the money in them. Again chant:

For the money that I need,

For the need that is so strong

For these words that I do read,

Brings the money right along.

Brings the money without waiting,

PARA-X POWERS

Brings the money right to me.

Brings the answer to my waiting,

Suddenly I will be free.

Close your eyes and place your fingertips on your temples and again see the money in your possession. After a few moments of this visualization, open your eyes again and chant:

Suddenly I see the pile,

Suddenly I hold the sum,

Suddenly I end my trial,

For the money—it has come!

PARA-X ENERGY WORD TO BRING ALL DESIRES

Certain sounds create unique energetic vibrations. These vibrations seek similar vibrations within the astral world, becoming a single creative force of energy that goes to work to make a physical manifestation of its power.

The secret chant I will soon reveal to you is so effective that it should be used with caution. I discovered it in a long out of print book of magic. I began using it, idly, without thinking and as I did, a strange sequence of events followed that even I am at a loss to explain. In the days and weeks ahead, everything I wanted I received with this secret chant; new friends, rare books, money, and more. I felt a strange sensation envelop me, a feeling of power and protection.

The chant should be spoken aloud in a sort of "up and down" rhythm. Before you begin saying the chant, practice aloud by counting from one to seven in the same voice that you will use when using the chant to influence chance and coincidence to bring you whatever it is you seek. As you practice, you will notice that you are developing a very definite rhythm as you pronounce the numbers. This same rhythm should be used as you use the chant. You are now ready to begin. Begin by using the concentration and

PARA-X POWERS

visualization techniques described in earlier chapters. You must clearly focus on what you desire, what you want to happen, etc.

Once you have clearly defined within your mind what you want, chant the Para-X Energy Word: <u>MISABU</u> (pronounced: ME-SAH-BOO) over and over again for at least five minutes. Ideally, the chant should begin as a shout and gradually fade away to a whisper.

THE GOLDEN SQUARE

Imagine a golden square directly in front of you. Now enlarge the image until it is several feet high, and pulsating with Para-X Power. See it as clearly as you can. Imagine yourself bathed in its mystic light. Try and actually breathe in this light. Imagine it circulating within you.

Now, in your mind, pretend that you are reaching into the golden square. Feel around inside until your hands touch two moneybags, bulging with gold coins. Pick the bags up and bring them out of the golden square.

Feel the coins with your mind, get involved with the coins, they're real. Repeat for seven consecutive days, or until the money arrives.

WOMAN USES GOLDEN SQUARE TO PAY BILL

This particular use of Para-X Power to bring money has proven to be very successful. Take for instance a friend of mine named Rita. One day she received an unexpected bill and had no idea where she could get the needed money. She was at her wit's end. So when I suggested that she use the Golden Square to draw money to her, she was only too happy to give it a try.

She followed my instructions and one week later, Laura's Grandmother came to visit and handed her an envelope. A gift, she told Laura. It contained $300 in cash.

CREATE YOUR OWN POWERFUL MONEY MAGNET

Para-X Power can be used to energize any small object so that you can carry with you at all times a powerful magnet to attract whatever you desire. Since this chapter is about money, let's make a Para-X Power Money Magnet.

PARA-X POWERS

To help form the proper impression in your mind and thus giving your Para-X Power a template to build on, pick something that represents money to you: a coin, something made from a precious metal, a piece of jewelry, etc. Don't forget to pick something small that can be easily carried in your pocket or purse.

Take an ordinary magnet, even a small magnet from your refrigerator will work, and rub it over your good luck money charm. The magnet symbolizes the money drawing capacity that your Para-X Money Magnet will now have. Now, say out loud to your Money Magnet:

Wealth, wealth, is drawn to me,
I deserve prosperity.
Rich I'll be,
money and prosperity are attracted to me.

Your Para-X Money Magnet is now charged and ready to start attracting money and good fortune to you 24 hours a day.

THE AMAZING PARA-TRANSMITTER

Look around you...do you realize that existing right along side this world there are a number of other realities? Science has shown that physical reality makes up only a small percentage of the Universe. The other, mysterious and unknown percentages are called Dark Matter and Dark Energy. Contained within these strange realms are what occultists have for centuries called the astral worlds; invisible worlds which seem to be the framework around which our own world is built.

You need to know this because right now, everything you need is in these invisible worlds, money, success, jewels, everything is waiting for you to call upon it, waiting for you to teleport it into existence in this world, to materialize into solid reality that you can see and touch.

All you need to make this happen is an amazing psychic tool, the amazing Para-Transmitter. With it, you can teleport the object of your desire to you, from the astral worlds.

This object, or person, or whatever you desire, is in its transparent state, called a Para-Form. The Para-Transmitter brings this object into focus, and photographs it psychically. Once this happens, it slowly materializes and becomes visible for you to see, feel, touch and possess.

PARA-X POWERS

The Para-Transmitter, like a magnifying glass, concentrates your thoughts and sends them like a burning streak of lightning to their destination. The Para-Transmitter is so amazingly simple that you will slap yourself for not thinking of it yourself. Before you beat yourself up, know that the Para-Transmitter has been around for centuries under various different names. It has been kept a closely guarded secret by those who want to keep this fantastic power exclusively for themselves. Do you think that many of the world's rich and powerful families got that way through hard work? No, they learned a long time ago some of the secrets of the occult world, such as how to use the Para-Transmitter, and made themselves rich beyond their wildest dreams.

Can the Para-Transmitter do this for you? It can, as long as you are willing to let go of your negative thoughts and are willing to dedicate the time to make your desires a reality.

The Para-Transmitter is constructed and used in the following manner. Take a large sheet of paper and roll it in the form of a funnel or cone, big enough to look through the wide end with both your eyes. The inside surface of this funnel should be blank. It is a scientific fact that such a device will direct your eyes to the other (narrow) end and restrict your vision to a very small area.

This psychic device may now be used as an aid to help you see and hear beyond barriers such as walls, floors, ceilings and doors...locate hidden treasures and large sums of money...or actually hear the thoughts of others.

Your Para-Transmitter now becomes a kind of magic or psychic camera when used to teleport the object of your desire to you, from the invisible world. To use it for this purpose, write down on a piece of white paper what it is that you desire. Be clear, precise and as descriptive as possible what it is that you want to happen. Write or print neatly (not too large) or use your computer and print out your message. Keep the messages short and clear.

Place the paper with your message before you on a table. Sit near it on a chair and hold the funnel, broad end to your eyes. The whole purpose of the funnel is to shut from your view the surrounding objects and to assist you in the concentration of your vision upon the message. By looking at it constantly you will see the message growing dim and indistinct. But do not allow such a thing to take place; by moving the pupils of the eye to and fro within the range of the paper you can avoid the blurring. In this experiment, the eye should not be allowed to grow fatigued. In case it shows any such fatigue, you should wink your eyes as often as possible.

PARA-X POWERS

It may not look like much, but the Para-Transmitter is an absolutely amazing device meant to focus your thought-waves into a laser-like beam of concentrated Para-X energy. The Para-Transmitter is constructed by taking a large sheet of paper, rolling it in the form of a funnel or cone, big enough to look through the wide end with both your eyes. It is a scientific fact that such a device will direct your eyes to the other (narrow) end and restrict your vision to a very small area. Now, write down on a piece of white paper what it is that you desire. By concentrating only on a small part of your message at a time, the psychic energies are increased.

PARA-X POWERS

When you use the Para-Transmitter this way, this psychic camera photographs its invisible, protoplasmic form, which then slowly becomes visible in the real world. When you concentrate on your message, you bring your desire into sharp, clear focus. You photograph it psychically, at which point it must materialize. (For this is the actual Law of Creation of the Universal Mind.) To give you an idea of how you should write your message, here are two examples of successful psychic messages transmitted to the astral worlds.

MONEY TRANSMISSION

Please bless me with new prosperity and a sudden increase in abundance. Starting now, and continuing for the rest of my days, let a golden river of glittering money pour into my life, filling it with sunshine, happiness and contentment. Let everything I touch turn to gold, and every enterprise or endeavor in which I am involved bring me the maximum rewards, without risk or loss of any kind. Shower me with my every want for as long as I remain worthy. Let life make known unto me its joys, its happiness. Let life reveal to me the fruits of my faith, the ripe, rich, succulent fruits of good fortune. Let it provide to me these offerings, for me to pluck to my heart's delight – to taste and savor endlessly for the rest of my days. For I am a good person, and will conduct myself in a manner worthy of the good fortune with which I am to be blessed – sharing and helping others along the way. Let me therefore know, now, any and all luxuries which I envision for I am a true believer in the maxim, "If there is any good I can do my fellow man, let me do it now, for I shall pass this way but once."

FIND THE PERFECT LOVE TRANSMISSION

Let me find my perfect mate, soon. Let them be drawn to me as the tide cleaves unto the shore. For this is a time for love. This is the time for desire. The single person who utters these words, alone or apart in spirit, desires a mate to satisfy the needs and fill the emptiness of my life. By these special words, let the perfect mate come rushing into my life. Let this person possess all the qualities that I desire (mention what you want of him or her). And let me possess all the qualities that this person desires. Let us be drawn to each other – though strangers we are now – by the invisible attractions of our strengths and weaknesses, and by the powerful desires which we express here and now. Let each of us be the perfect mate in the other's eyes.

WOMAN FINDS LOST MONEY WITH PARA-TRANSMITTER

Christine M., a widow, says she felt silly using the Para-Transmitter, but thought it was worth a try, since she had a family to support. She happened to be holding her checkbook in her hand – she was always paying bills – when she transmitted a money message. When she looked around and saw nothing, she thought, "Well, it serves me right." A short time later, however, when her monthly bank statement arrived, she happened to notice a balance $100 higher than her checkbook showed. Was it luck or coincidence? Apparently, in the normal routine of checking, the bank had corrected a simple arithmetical error that she had made.

MAN FINDS THE PERFECT HOME WITH PARA-TRANSMITTER

George W. thought that he would never own his own home. For a large part of his life he could only manage to afford the rent for an apartment. When he discovered how to construct the Para-Transmitter, he considered that he didn't have anything to lose, and gave it a try. George spent several days writing down everything that he wanted in a new house. How it would look, where it was located, what kind of furniture it would have inside. He did not leave out a single detail for his dream home. For days after he transmitted his new home message, he continued to concentrate on bringing his new home into physical reality. He never wavered in believing that his desire for a new home would eventually happen. Then, several weeks later, George was unexpectedly offered a management position at his job. His new position came with a large increase in salary, enough for him to be able to build his dream home, exactly as he had envisioned in his Para-Transmission.

8
HEALING WITH PARA-X POWERS

THERE is no phase of psychic influence that is more familiar to the average person of the Western world than the healing of physical ills and conditions by means of psychic influence under one name or another. Great healing cults and organizations have been built up upon this basis, and the interest in the subject has taken on the form of a great popular movement.

As is natural in cases of this kind, there have been hundreds of theories advanced to account for the phenomena of psychic, or Para-X Healing, and a still greater number of methods of treatments devised to carry out the principles of the theories. Ranging from the teaching of actual divine interposition and influence arising from certain forms of belief and practice, covering many intermediate stages, the theories even include a semi-materialistic hypothesis in which mind is considered as an attribute of matter, but having a magic influence over the forms of matter when properly applied. But it is worthy of note that no matter what the general or particular theory, or what the favored method of application, these healing schools or cults, as well as the independent practitioners, meet with a very fair degree of success and perform quite a number of cures.

Many of these Western advocates and practitioners of psychic healing practically hold that the whole system is of very recent discovery, and that it has nothing whatsoever to do with ordinary occult science. The occultists however are able to smile at these ideas and beliefs, for they not only recognize the general principles involved, but they also are aware that Para-X Healing and its application, have been known to advanced occultists for thousands of years. I do not say this in any disparagement of the modern schools of psychic healing, for I am in full sympathy with their great work; I merely mention the matter that the student may get the right historical perspective in considering this phase of psychic phenomena and influence.

So far as the methods of application are concerned, the true occultist recognizes that most of the methods and forms of treatment are but outward cloaks or disguises for the real psychic healing principle. The gist of the real methods is to be found in the principles of the application of Para-X Powers: (1) Strong desire to make the cure; (2) clear mental image or picture of the desired condition as actually present in the patient at this time; and (3) concentration of the attention and mind of the healer, so as to bring to a focus to two preceding mental states.

PARA-X POWERS

Here you have the real secret of Para-X Healing methods, the rest are all elaborations, dressed up forms and ceremonies which affect the imagination, faith, belief and confidence of the patient, and thus make the healing process much easier. In fact, with the proper degree of faith and confidence on the part of the patient, there is but little need of a healer, for the patient may treat and cure himself. However, in most cases, the presence of the healer aids materially in arousing the fate and confidence of the patient, and hastens the cure.

Again, so far as the theories underlying the cures are concerned, occultists are able to reduce them all to a single working theory or principle, which includes all the rest. Brushing aside all technical details, and all attempts to trace back the healing process to the ultimate facts of the universe, I may say that the gist of the principle of Para-X Healing is that of influencing the astral foundation of the various organs and parts, cells and centers, so as to make it proceed to manifest a more perfect physical counterpart.

All Para-X Healing is really accomplished on the astral body first, and then the physical body responds to the renewed activities of its astral counterpart. To get the real significance of this statement it is necessary for you to realize just what the astral body really is. This once grasped, the difficulties vanish, and you are able to form a clear conception of the entire matter and process.

The astral body is a precise counterpart of the physical body, its organs, its parts, its centers, and its cells. In fact, the astral body is the pattern upon which the physical body is materialized. The astral body is composed of an etheric substance of a very high rate of vibration. In one sense it may be considered as a very subtle form of matter, in another as a semi-materialized form of force or energy. It is finer and more subtle that the rarest vapors or gases known to science. And, yet, it has a strong degree of tenacity and cohesiveness that enables it to resist attacks from the material side of nature.

As I have said, each organ, part, center or cell, of the physical body has its astral pattern or basis. In fact, the physical body has been built up, in whole and in all of its parts, on the pattern and base of the astral body. Moreover, in case of impaired functioning of the physical organs or parts, and impaired activity of the physical body, its limbs, etc., if we can manage to arouse the activities of the astral body we may cause it to re-materialize or re-energize the physical body, and thus restore health and activity to it.

If the liver, for instance, is not functioning properly, we proceed to start up the activities of the astral counterpart of that organ, to the end that the physical organ may be re-energized, and recreated in a measure. All true Para-X Healing work is performed on the astral plane, before it manifests on the physical.

PRANA – THE LIFE ENERGY

At this point, I should also call your attention to the effect of "prana," or life energy, in some cases of healing. This prana is what Western healers mean when they speak of "human magnetism" in their healing work. So far from being an imaginary force, as claimed by the physical scientists and materialists, it is known to all occultists as an active principle of the human body, and as of great efficacy in the psychic treatment of disease.

Before passing on to the consideration of other phases of the subject before us, I would like to call your attention to the fact that from the earliest days of history there have been recorded instances of some form of psychic healing. In the earlier days the psychic healing work was left entirely in the hands of the priesthood of the various religions prevailing in the several counties of the world.

Claiming to have an exclusive divine sanction to perform healing work, these priests used various ceremonies, rites, incantations, etc., in order to obtain their results. In many cases these priests were ignorant of the real psychic forces invoked and set into operation; they merely practiced methods which had been found to work out effectively, and which had been handed down to them by their predecessors. In other cases, however, the priests undoubtedly were skilled occultists, and had a very full knowledge of the forces they were using; though, as the masses of the people were very ignorant it was impossible to acquaint them with these things so far above their understanding; and, consequently, the priests applied the healing forces under the disguise of their religious ceremonies and rites.

From time to time, however, as civilization progressed, there came into prominence persons who worked cures of physical ills by means of magical ceremonies and other similar methods, but who were outside of the priesthood. Some of these men undoubtedly had a very fair knowledge of the real secret of their cures, though they disguised them to suit the mental condition of their patients, and, also, probably for purposes of self glorification.

In other cases, however, it is probable that these healers had merely stumbled across the fact that certain things said in a certain way tended to work cures; or that certain physical objects seemed to have therapeutic virtue. They did not realize that the whole healing virtue of their systems depended upon the strong idea in their own minds, coupled with the strong faith and confidence in the mind of the patient. And so the work went on.

LAYING ON OF HANDS

In some of the oldest records of the human race, the scriptures of the various peoples, we find that "laying on of hands" was the favorite method employed by the holy men and priests, and other performing healing work. From the first there seems to have been an almost instinctive recognition on the part of man of the fact that there is a healing power in the touch of the hand.

Mothers instinctively apply their hands to the hurt bodies of their children – a custom that can be found all over the world. The child is taught to expect physical relief from the application of the mother's hands, and its mind at once pictures relief. Not only is the mental picture created, but the desire and confidence is established in the minds of both persons.

The same thing is true of all "laying on of hands," and thus are the principles of all psychic influence brought into play. But this is not all there is to it. In the first place, there is an actual transference of prana from the body of the healer to that of the patient, which serves to energize and revitalize the cells and centers of the body of the latter. In the second place, there is the effect upon the astral body of the patient, which tends to materialize better physical conditions. In the third place, there is that combination and union of the minds of the two persons, which gives extra force and power to psychic influence. Is it any wonder that cures take place under these circumstances?

In the modern revival of the almost lost art and science of Para-X Healing among the general public, there has been unusual stress laid upon the feature of "absent healing," in which the patient and the healer are not in each other's presence. To many this has seemed actually miraculous, and as a positive proof of divine interposition. But a little thought will show the student that such cures are not unknown in the pages of history, as a casual examination of the sacred books of almost any religion will show. Moreover, the student will see that to the effect of certain principles of Para-X Powers, there needs but to be added the principles of telepathic communication, or, better still, the principles of astral communication by some phases of clairvoyance, to account for the entire phenomena of "absent healing."

For Para-X Powers, space and time is no barrier on the astral plane. Once the en rapport condition is established between healer and patient, and the rest is simple – the astral body is induced to energize more actively, and as a result the physical manifestation is improved and normal functioning restored.

In cases of Para-Healing, the healer by an effort of his will (sometimes unconsciously applied) projects a supply of his pranic aura vibrations into the body of his patient, by way of the nervous system of the patient, and also by means of what may be called the induction of the aura itself. The mere presence of a person strongly charged with prana, is often enough to cause an overflow into the aura of other persons, with a resulting feeling of new strength and energy.

By the use of the hands of the healer, a heightened effect is produced, by reason of certain properties inherent in the nervous system of both healer and patient. There is even a flow of etheric substance from the aura of the healer to that of the patient, in cases in which the vitality of the latter is very low. Many a healer has actually, and literally, pumped his life force and etheric substance into the body of his patient, when the latter was sinking into the weakness which precedes death, and has by so doing been able to bring him back to strength and life. This is practically akin to the transfusion of blood — except that it is upon the psychic plane instead of the physical.

HEALING MIND, BODY AND SOUL

While treating his patients by the laying on of hands, a healer strives to induce in the mind of the patient the mental image of restored health and physical strength; he pictures the diseased organ as restored to health and normal functioning; he sees the entire physiological machinery operating properly, the work of nutrition, assimilation, and excretion going on naturally and normally. By proper words of advice and encouragement he awakens hope and confidence in the mind of the patient, and thus obtains the cooperation of that mind in connection to his own mental efforts. The astral body responds to this treatment, and begins to energize the physical organs and cells into normal activity and the journey toward health is begun.

In the form of psychic treatment which comes under the head of Suggestive Therapeutics, great insistence is laid upon the verbal suggestion to the patient, on the part of the healer. The patient is told that he will get well; that his organs will function normally; etc., etc.

The power of the spoken word evokes and induces the mental image of the desired condition in the mind of the patient. The mental picture produces a corresponding effect in the astral body of the patient, and sets into operation the materialization of desired results. In addition, the words produce a strong mental picture in the mind of the healer himself, and thus give form and strength to his psychic vibrations which are being poured out toward the patient.

If you wish to treat yourself for some physical disorder, or if you wish to help others in the same way, you have but to put into operation the general principles of Para-Healing. You must first be filled with the strong desire and wish to make the cure; then you must make a strong mental image of the desired result, as actually present. (Do not think of it as "going to be;" instead say and think that it "is now!"); then concentrate the attention firmly and positively upon the idea.

You may aid yourself and others by affirmations or auto-suggestions (words creating desired ideas and mental pictures) if you wish – you may get better results in this way. In this connection, let me remind you that the healing work in many cases consists largely in placing proper mental pictures in the mind of the patient, thereby displacing improper and harmful mental pictures of disease, etc., which have been given lodgment there before.

Many persons are sick because of improper and harmful mental pictures that they have allowed to be placed there by the suggestions of others. Fear and dread of disease often acts to bring about the feared condition, for reasons that you can readily see.

USING PARA-HEALING AT A DISTANCE

As stated earlier, time and space have no effect on Para-X Powers. In order to use Para-Healing for someone who is quite a distance away from you, first sit quietly in your own room, inducing a calm, peaceful mental attitude and state. Then make a mental picture of the patient as sitting opposite to you, or lying down in front of you. If you have never seen the patient, make simply a mental image of a man, or a woman, as the case may be, and think of the figure as being the patient. The best practitioners of distant psychic healing produce such a strong mental image of the patient that they can often actually "feel" his or her presence. (This of course is the result of a simple form of clairvoyance.)

Next, make a strong mental picture of the condition that you wish to induce in the patient, the healthy physical condition of the organ, or part or body, as the case may be. See this condition as existing at the present time, and not as merely to come in the future. At the same time, you will do well to mentally speak to the patient, just as you would in case he or she was sitting before you

PARA-X POWERS

in the physical body. Tell the patient just what you would in such case. Pour in the suggestions, or affirmations, or whatever you may wish to call them. In some cases in which an excellent en rapport condition is established, patients become aware of the treatment, and sometimes can almost see and feel the presence of the healer.

Make sure to consider each of the organs of the patient, or of themselves, as having a separate intelligence; and, therefore, to "speak up to it" as if it really understood what was being said to its organ-mind. The principle of concentration and mental picturing is invoked very strongly and the astral counterpart of the organ should respond to such treatment quickly and effectively.

It is a fact that there is mind in every organ and cell of the body, and if the same is awakened in the astral counterpart, it will respond to the command, suggestion, or direction. Finally, no matter what may be the theory, or method, given in connection with psychic healing of any or all kinds, you will find the same general principles underlying it that have been presented over and over again in this book. In fact, many purely material and physical remedies owe their success to the fact that they appeal to the imagination of the patient, and also inspire confidence in him.

Anything that will inspire confidence, faith and hope in the mind of a patient, and will bring to his mind strong mental pictures of restored health and normal functioning of his organs, that thing will make for health for him.

PARA-X POWERS

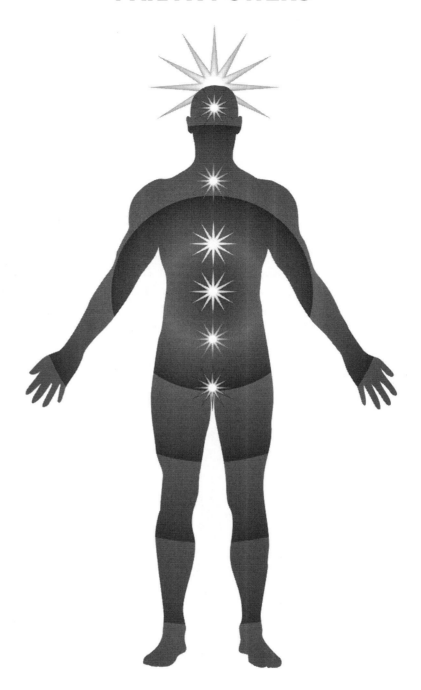

Each organ, part, center or cell of the physical body has an astral pattern. Para-X Healing is thus performed on the astral plane before it manifests itself upon the physical.

PARA-X POWERS

9
PARA-VIEW INTO THE
PAST, PRESENT, AND FUTURE

THERE is a fantastic ability with Para-X Powers that allows you to easily see into the past, present and even the future. This ability is as easy to accomplish as sitting down and turning on your High Definition television set. But your HDTV won't allow you to see hidden secrets from the past, nor will it allow you to see what others are thinking about right at this very moment. Plus, I doubt that your TV has the ability to catch glimpses of the many probabilities of the future.

This valuable technique derived from Para-X Powers is called The Para-Viewer and it uses the reflective and refractive properties of a sphere made of crystal or glass in order to receive transmissions from the astral worlds. Of course this device is better known as a crystal ball, but a Para-Viewer can also be any object that is shiny and reflective, a mirror, or a clear glass of water for example.

For centuries people have been using crystal balls in an attempt to get a look into the future. This is a form of fortune telling called Scrying. The stereotype of an old Gypsy woman using a crystal ball to cheat a customer out of his hard-earned money has become so ingrained upon society that most people automatically reject the idea that a crystal ball has any valid psychic uses at all.

But don't let the bad publicity turn you away from learning how to use this amazing and useful device. The Para-Viewer can become an important tool for your success in business, love and all sorts of other major decisions in your life.

Man has made a considerable advance on the road to Attainment. Self-development and self-initiation are beginning to play a much more prominent part than before. Man is no longer content to believe what he is told; he at last desires to know from his own experience. The Para-Viewer is a vital stepping-stone towards self-knowledge.

Crystal gazing, as a method for inducing visions, has been quite common among all peoples, in all times. Not only the crystal but many other objects are similarly used; in Australia the native priests use water and shining objects, or in some cases, flame. In New Zealand some of the natives use a drop of blood. The Fijians fill a hole with water, and gaze into it. Some South American tribes use the polished surface of a black stone. The Native Americans used water and shining bits of flint or quartz.

PARA-X POWERS

A Para-Viewer can be any object that is shiny and reflective, a crystal sphere, a mirror, or a clear glass of water.

PARA-X POWERS

YOUR PARA-VIEWER

The first thing you need to do is to find a Para-Viewer that you like and are comfortable using. Some esoteric scholars insist that only pure quartz crystal can be used for psychic viewing. This is only true if you believe it to be true. Nowadays there are many different types of materials that are used to make "crystal" balls...each and every one of them will work for you if you believe it will. That is why it is important to find one that appeals to you. In fact, look for a Para-Viewer that draws you to it like a piece of metal to a magnet. Then you will know for certain that you have found the right one.

The Occult Teachings inform us that in addition to the Five Physical Senses possessed by man: Seeing; Feeling; Hearing; Tasting; and Smelling; each of which has its appropriate sense organ, every individual is also possessed of Five Astral Senses, which form a part of what is known to Occultists as the Astral Body. These Astral Senses, which are the astral counterparts of the five physical senses, operate upon what

Occultists call the Astral Plane, which is next above the Physical Plane, in the Sevenfold Scale of Planes. Just as do the Physical Senses operate upon the Physical Plane, so do the Astral Senses operate upon the Astral Plane. By means of these Astral Senses, one may sense outside objects without the use of the physical senses usually employed. And it is through this sensing by these Astral Senses, that the phenomenon of Para-Viewing becomes possible.

By the employment of the Astral Sense of Seeing, the Para-Viewer is able to perceive occurrences, scenes, etc., at a distance sometimes almost incredibly far; to see through solid objects; to see records of past occurrences in the Astral Ether; and to see Future Scenes thrown ahead in Time, like the shadows cast by material objects — "coming events cast their shadows before," you have heard. By the use of the Astral Sense of Hearing, he is able to sense sounds over immense distances and often after the passage of great periods of time, for the Astral vibrations continue for many years.

The Astral senses of Taste and Smell are seldom used, although there are abundant proofs of their existence. The Astral Sense of Feeling enables the Para-Viewer to become aware of certain occurrences on the Astral Plane, and to perceive impressions, mental and otherwise, that are being manifested at a distance.

PARA-X POWERS

The Astral Sense of Feeling may be explained as being rather a sense of "Awareness," than a mere "Feeling," inasmuch as the viewer, through its channel, becomes "aware" of certain occurrences, other than by Astral Sight or Hearing, and yet which is not "Feeling" as the word is used on the Physical Plane. It may be well called "Sensing" for want of a better name, and manifests in a vague consciousness or "awareness."

Still, we must not overlook the fact that there are many instances of true "feeling" on the Astral Plane, for instances, cases where the viewer actually "feels" the pain of another, which phenomena is commonly known as "sympathetic pains," "taking on the condition," etc., etc., and which are well known to all investigators as belonging to the phenomena of the Astral Senses.

HOW TO DEVELOP YOURSELF

The ability to Para-View lies dormant in every person. This means that the Astral Senses are present in everyone, and the possibility of their being awakened into activity is always present. The different degrees of power observable in different persons depend chiefly upon the degree of development rather than upon the comparative strength of the faculties. In some persons, of certain temperaments, the Astral Senses are very near the manifesting point at all times.

Flashes of what are considered to be "intuition," premonitions, etc., are really manifestations of Para-X Powers in some phase. In the case of other persons, on the other hand, the Astral Senses are almost atrophied, so merged in materialistic thought and life are these people. The element of Faith also plays an important point in this phenomenon, as it does in all occult phenomena, for that matter. That is to say, that one's belief tends to open up the latent powers and faculty in man, while a corresponding disbelief tends to prevent the manifestation.

There is a very good psychological reason for this as all students of the subject well know. Belief and Disbelief are two potent psychological factors on all planes of action. Occultists know, and teach, that the Astral Senses and faculties of the human race will unfold as the race progresses, at which time that which we now call Para-X Power will be a common possession of all persons, just as the use of the physical senses are to the race at the present time. In the meantime, there are persons who, not waiting for the evolution of the race, are beginning to manifest this power in a greater or lesser degree, depending much upon favorable circumstances, etc.

PARA-X POWERS

There are many more persons in this stage of development than is generally realized. In fact many persons manifesting Para-X Power, occasionally, are apt to pass by the phenomena as "imagination," and "foolishness," refusing to recognize its reality.

Then, again, many persons manifest the power during sleeping hours, and dismiss the matter as "merely a dream," etc.

You may ask "how will I know when my psychic abilities with the Para-Viewer begin to work?"

Some people begin by a plunge, as it were, and under some unusual stimulus become able just for once to see some striking vision; and very often in such a case, because the experience does not repeat itself, the seer comes in time to believe that on that occasion he must have been the victim of hallucination. Others begin by becoming intermittently conscious of the brilliant colors and vibrations of the human aura; others find themselves with increasing frequency seeing and hearing something to which those around them are blind and deaf; others again see faces, landscapes, or colored clouds floating before their eyes in the dark, before they sink to rest; while perhaps the commonest experience of all is that of those who begin to recollect with greater and greater clearness what they have seen and heard on other planes during sleep.

While it is very difficult to lay down a set method of instruction in the development of your ability to use your Para-Viewer, there are some things that are generally important for anyone seeking to develop their Para-X Powers.

The first is concentration. You should cultivate the faculty of concentration, which is the power to hold the attention upon an object for some time. Very few possess this power, although they may think they do. The best way to develop concentration is to practice on some familiar and common object, such as a pencil, book, ornament, etc. Take up the object and study it in detail, forcing the mind to examine and consider it in every part, until every detail of the object has been observed and noted. Then lay the object aside, and a few hours after pick it up again and repeat the process, and you will be surprised to see how many points you have missed on the first trial, Repeat this until you feel that you have exhausted your object. The next day take up another object, and repeat the process.

Practicing this way will not only greatly develop the powers of Perception, but will also strengthen your powers of concentration in a manner which will be of great value to you in Para-X development.

The second point of development is visualizing. In order to visualize you must cultivate the faculty of forming mental pictures of distant scenes, places, people, etc., until you can summon them before you at will, when you place yourself in the proper mental condition.

Another plan is to place yourself in a comfortable position, and then make a mental journey to some place that you have previously visited. Prepare for the journey, and then mentally see yourself starting on your trip; then seeing all the intermediate places and points; then arriving at your destination and visiting the points of interest, etc.; and then returning home. Then, later try to visit places that you have never seen, in the same way. This is not clairvoyance, but is a training of the mental faculties for the exercise of the real power.

After you have developed yourself along the lines of concentration, and visualization as above stated, you may begin to practice Psychometry, as follows: Take a lock of hair; or handkerchief; or ribbon; or ring; belonging to some other person, and then press it against your forehead, lightly, closing your eyes, and assuming a receptive and passive mental state. Then desire calmly that you Psychometrize the past history of the object. Do not be in too much of a hurry, but await calmly the impressions.

After a while you will begin to receive impressions concerning the person owning the object pressed against your forehead. You will form a mental picture of the person, and will soon begin to receive impressions about his characteristics, etc.

You may practice with a number of objects, at different times, and will gradually develop the Psychometric power by such practice and experiments. Remember that you are developing what is practically a new sense, and must have perseverance and patience in educating and unfolding it.

Another form of Para-X development is that of tracing the past history, surroundings, etc., of metals, minerals, etc. The process is identical to that just described. The mineral is pressed against the forehead, and with closed eyes the person awaits the Psychometric impression.

Some who have highly developed the faculty have been able to describe the veins of mineral, metal, etc., and to give much valuable information regarding same, all arising from the psychic clue afforded by a sample of the rock, mineral, metal, etc. There are other cases of record, in which underground streams of water have been discovered by Psychometrists, by means of the clue given by a bit of earth, stone, etc., from the surface. In this, as in the other phase mentioned, practice, practice, practice, is the summing up of the instruction regarding development.

PARA-X POWERS

LOOK INTO YOUR PARA-VIEWER

Now that you are ready to gaze for the first time into your Para-Viewer, you should select a quiet room where you will be entirely undisturbed, taking care that it is as far as possible free from mirrors, ornaments, pictures, glaring colors and the like, which may otherwise distract the attention.

This room should be of a comfortable temperature in accordance with the time of year, neither too hot nor too cold. Make sure to prevent any artificial light rays from being reflected in, or in any manner directly reaching your Para-Viewer. Keep any light source to your back. The room should not be dark, but rather shadowed, or charged with dull light, somewhat such as prevails on a cloudy or wet day.

The Para-Viewer should be placed on a table, or it may rest on a dark colored cloth. Just make sure that there are no undesirable reflections to disturb your viewing. Before beginning to experiment, remember that most frequently nothing will be seen on the first occasion, and possibly not for several sittings, though some sitters, if strongly gifted with psychic powers may be fortunate enough to obtain good results the very first time.

For your first few times, have no goals set, simply gaze calmly at the Para-Viewer. Do not be afraid of blinking your eyes, and do not stare, strain or tire the eyes. Some prefer making funnels of their hands, and gazing through them as this serves to shut out distracting light, and sights. (You can use your Para-Transmitter for this purpose).

If nothing is perceived during the first few attempts, do not despair or become impatient or imagine that you will never see anything. Using your Para-Viewer is like learning to ride a bike, you may fall off the first few times, but eventually you will succeed.

It has been recommended that beginners failing to get direct results then try to "visualize" something that they have already seen something familiar, such as a chair, a ring, a face, etc., and then turning to the Para-Viewer and try to reproduce it there. It is claimed that this practice will often gradually lead to actual "seeing" in the Para-Viewer.

The first signs of the actual "seeing" in the Para-Viewer comes in the form of a "cloudiness," or "milky-mist," which slowly resolves itself into a form, or scene, which slowly appears within your Para-Viewer. In some cases, the "misty" cloud deepens into a black one, from which the pictures appear.

The Para-Viewer shouldn't be used right after eating, and avoid alcoholic drinks before a session. The proper state of mind when using the Para-Viewer is extremely important. Mental anxiety, or ill health will play havoc with your sessions, so if you do not feel good, postpone your Para-Viewer session until later.

Some experts say that when you do start to see images within your Para-Viewer as a general rule, visions appearing in the extreme background indicate the far past or far future. While those images seen neared to the front denote the present or immediate future.

This question of "time" is an important one, and it is unfortunate that it should largely depend on your hunch. Time on other planes of reality is different from our own time. Since time is a mode of the human mind, and our mind is at a different state of vibration when examining a vision, the question is can you discern what "time" you are actually looking at? I think the best rule with this is to depend on your first impressions as these usually are correct. As you become more proficient at reading your Para-Viewer you will just "know" what you are looking at and at what "time" it is taking place.

UNDERSTANDING SYMBOLS

You will see two principal types of visions with your Para-Viewer: (1) The Symbolic, indicated by the appearance of symbols such as a flag, boat, knife, gold, etc.: and (2) Actual scenes and people, in action or otherwise.

Symbols are thought-forms which convey, by the association of ideas, a definite meaning in regard to the mind that generates them. They depend upon the laws of thought, and the correspondence that exists between the spiritual and material worlds, between the subject and the object of our consciousness.

All symbols, therefore, may be translated by reference to the known nature, quality, and uses of the objects they represent. Thus an arm will signify defense, power, protection; a mouth speech, revelation; an ear news, information; if distorted, scandal, abuse. The sun, shining brightly, denotes prosperity, honors. The moon, when crescent denotes success, increase, and improvement. When gibbous, it denotes sickness, losses, and trouble. The sun eclipsed shows death or ruin of a man; the moon, similarly afflicted, denotes equal danger to a woman. These are natural interpretations.

Symbols are almost infinite in number, and the interpretation of them requires unprejudiced skill, but they are nevertheless an important subject for study, and the use of the Crystal or Mirror by a positive seer can hardly be beneficial without a profound understanding of this subject. Although every symbol has some general signification in agreement with its natural qualities and uses, yet it obtains a particular meaning in relation to the individual. This is also the case in dreams, where every person is a natural seer. Few, however, pay that attention to dreams which their source and nature warrant. The Para-Viewer is but a means of bringing the normal dreaming faculty into conscious activity.

No definite rule can be laid down as to the interpretation of visions. The answers are actually within you. Your own personal symbols, as interpreted by your subconscious mind, are what you will end up viewing. If you associate airplanes with having to travel a great distance because of a death in the family, then when you see the image of an airplane in your Para-Viewer you are going to think of death and sorrow.

If you associate roller skating with meeting your first girl or boy friend, then if you experience a vision of people roller skating in your Para-Viewer, you are going to think of love and romance. So pay attention to how these images make you feel deep inside when you see them. Chances are the feelings; the very emotions that these symbols evoke within you are going to be the correct interpretations.

WOMAN FINDS LOST PET WITH PARA-VIEWER

One person who became convinced that her Para-Viewer did actually work was Annie G. of Nashville, Tennessee. Annie had been drawn to a small, glass ball that she found at an antique store. Right away she bought it, even though she really didn't need it. Later that week, Annie's beloved pet cat was accidentally let out of her apartment.

Annie was heartbroken and several days went by with no sign of her cat. Following the instructions on how to use a Para-Viewer, Annie sat down in a shaded room and concentrated on seeing her cat within her small, glass sphere.

Annie soon entered into a light trance state and her entire focus was on her little Para-Viewer. From within the clear, shiny ball, Annie could see an image slowly forming, it was the front entrance of a nearby convenience store.

She rushed to the store, and there was her cat. The owners had found her cat and were trying to find its owner. Somehow her Para-Viewer showed her a literal image on where Annie could find her cat. Annie's Para-Viewer was no fancy expensive crystal ball, but it worked just as well.

PARA-X POWERS

PARA-VIEWER FINDS MONEY

Jake S. was a construction worker until the recent economic hardships, especially in the housing market, forced Jake's company to lay him off. With a family to take care of, Jake was uncertain what to do next.

Jake decided to put together his own Para-Viewer using a clear drinking glass filled with fresh water. He sat in a dark room with the glass in front of him and a small candle placed several feet away and to the right of the glass.

The first time Jake sat and looked into the glass for ten minutes. He grew tired and bored and gave up for the rest of the day. Late that night, Jake woke up and could not go back to sleep. He decided that since he was already awake and didn't have anything else to do, he would give his Para-Viewer another try. This time, however, almost as soon as he sat down in front of the glass, unusual images seem to float before his eyes from deep within the water.

As the images took shape, Jake recognized an old car, a Chevy, that his parents had owned when he was a child. He always associated his late father with that car as it had been his father's favorite and the two of them would spend the weekend's together working on it in their old garage.

Jake could not understand what his father's old car had to do with his need for money. His father had passed away years before and the car was long gone. He decided to visit his old childhood home, now abandoned and marked to be torn down, and see if he could find anything that could help him out.

Jake wandered through his old home, but nothing of any significance stood out to him. He then went out to the old garage to look around. The garage was completely empty and Jake was about to leave when he noticed something written on the wall. It was both his and his father's signatures along with a date from years ago. Jake remembered that they had signed the wall in celebration after successfully rebuilding the carburetor of the old Chevy.

Jake fondly brushed his hand across the old writing, and when he did the board shifted and came away from the wall. Inside the space was a yellowed envelope with Jake's name written on it in his father's handwriting. Opening the envelope, Jake found a large amount of cash, enough to keep his family going until he could find a new job. Jake has no idea when or why his father had hidden the money, but, if it hadn't been for the image seen in his Para-Viewer, he never would have found the money that his father had tucked away for him years ago.

PARA-X POWERS

A FEW HELPFUL HINTS

This chapter, while giving as much information as possible in the space allowed, aims to be intensely practical and helpful to all who may read it. Some will be at one stage of development, others will have reached a different level, but the author trusts that all will obtain some hints that may actually be put into practice, and thus lead the seeker to a clearer and better understanding of himself and others.

Here are a few practical hints:

A diet of fruit and vegetables may have its advantages by making the student more susceptible to visions of a clairvoyant type. On the other hand a mixed diet suits some people far better, and may give more real staying power. Don't become a "diet crank" you will have no time for anything else more important. Use your common sense – experiment if you like – but don't form habits. The best type of man or woman is the one who can eat anything, and does eat anything according to the natural promptings of his or her being, and that without causing digestive troubles.

Don't do any practice after a full meal, or when very tired; this would not be giving Nature a proper chance, and your practice must suffer accordingly.

Rather be the tortoise than the hare. Real progress is made despite obstacles, and the more obstacles we meet, and overcome, the stronger our will becomes.

You are practically bound to obtain what you truly ask for. Be sure of what you really want before you ask for it.

Take plenty of fresh air and exercise, and don't become so obsessed with dark séances that you overlook the value of Sunlight.

Your first duty to Humanity is self-improvement. Man is ignorant of the nature and powers of his own being. Until he has obtained a scientific knowledge of himself, he cannot really expect to aid others.

It requires much more study and effort to Know Yourself, than it does to give others advice they do not need.

Learn to mind your own business, and in time others will follow your example.

PARA-X POWERS

Learn to speak the truth, and you will begin to notice when you are telling lies.

Remember that even truth is relative. There is but one Truth and that lies at the

End of the Path. Yet seek Truth, and be content with nothing less.

We live in a world of appearances. There seem to be innumerable, "Pairs of Opposites" till the final Pair has been realized and mated. Then we shall "See things as they are."

10
HOW TO HEAR SECRET MESSAGES FROM THE UNIVERSE WITH PARA-X POWERS

THROUGHOUT this book we have shown you how easy it is to use Para-X Powers to help you make your hearts desires a reality and to receive answers to your life-long questions. In this chapter we will show you how to use your Para-X Powers to learn how to listen for messages from the Universe that are being sent to help in your everyday life in the form of signs or suggestions.

These signs can take the form of dreams, omens, apparitions, feelings, natural phenomena, what other people say or do, even the behavior of animals. Universal signs always pint the way to opportunities, which if acted upon, literally push you ahead to success with little or no effort.

In this chapter, we shall see some of the ways the Universe reveals its signs to you. While it is not possible to predict the exact sign that will be revealed in a given situations, most cosmic signs and the circumstances under which they are revealed do have certain specific characteristics which it is possible to talk about. These include:

(1)   The Signs of love
(2)   The Signs of Prosperity
(3)   The Signs of Right
(4)   The Signs of Wrong
(5)   The Signs of Danger
(6)   The Signs of Salvation

ARE YOU LISTENING?

Are you listening? The Universe is sending you signs and omens to help point you in the right direction. There are a myriad of signs everywhere for the observant eye to behold. How you interpret the meaning of the signs you are shown is a personal thing wide open to interpretation, and misinterpretation. What one person may dismiss could be very important to another. For example, whenever a friend of mine sees a specific courier van, this signals that an invitation is on its way.

Some signs are obvious – their message is loud and clear. Others are more ambiguous. The Universe usually leaves you a trail of very subtle clues that are not easy to decipher, often being metaphorical or symbolic in nature. Symbols speak to your subconscious mind, and hold great potency and power.

An old Native American saying reads: *To look is one thing. To see what you look at is another. To understand what you see is a third. To learn from what you understand is still something else. But to act on what you learn is all that really matters!*

With Para-X Powers, there is a science, as well as an art, to reading signs and signals. Our beliefs and intentions go out from us and have an impact not only on other people, but also on what happens to us.

Signs and synchronicity are pure physics. All outer signs are a mirror reflection of our inner consciousness. The quantum mechanics of meaningful coincidences is constantly working for us. Our magnetic field of energy is always attracting exactly what we need to create our hearts' desires. We're destined to enjoy an abundant life—and the Universe is designed to help us find it.

You can successfully navigate through the myriad of your life choices by using the precise guidance system that the Astral world constantly presents. You can increase the number of fulfilling life opportunities by increasing the accuracy of your interpretations of signs. And you can open the door to more magic, meaning and money in your world by learning to suspend skepticism and conditioned responses.

All our emotions and dreams are encoded messages from the Universe. The soul also talks to us through inner and outer coded symbols, sounds and unusual lights, or intermediaries like angels and spirit guides. Often the soul has to resort to dramatic, external events to grab our attention, like body symptoms or car and computer trouble. When has your soul had to resort to strong tactics to get your attention? (For example, sickness, accident, divorce).

Life offers us a practical Early Warning System. That is if we pay attention and listen to what is being said to us. Life gives us messages. When we fail to get the message, life gives us a lesson. If we don't learn the lesson, life gives us a problem. If we don't deal with the problem, life gives us a crisis.

ARE YOU GETTING THE MESSAGE?

In many Native American languages, the word for "getting the message" is the same word used for "my life has changed." In other words, in their culture, if you don't act on the guiding signs presented by the Great Spirit, you didn't really get the message. If you don't make the necessary changes in your behavior and attitude to alter the course of your destiny, you never really understood the true import of the message.

Being in intimate touch with the ebb and flow of the interconnectedness of life, indigenous peoples recognize life's outer signals as useful Early Warning Signs. These outer signs are reflecting the inevitable outer course of our inner river of consciousness. Native peoples know the only way to have their life unfold harmoniously is to respond immediately to the accurate feedback life gives them. For indigenous people, there is no middle ground as there is for most modern, intellectual Westerners.

In modern times people often respond differently to divine assistance. Instead of responding immediately as would native peoples, contemporary Americans typically "think" about the signs being given by the Universe Even after recognizing the wisdom of the message, most people still don't make the indicated changes in their life. In allowing the thinking mind to enter into the equation, we invite misinterpretation, discounting, invalidation and even denial of the message. And most often, the result of this mental intervention is inaction. We always have our "good reasons" not to make the changes suggested by the Universe.

By following the techniques for Para-X Powers, as discussed in earlier chapters; concentration, visualization, attraction, you can open yourself up to be more vigilant to spot signs and opens that are trying to point you in the direction you need to go. As well, do not dismiss events that involve coincidence. There is no such thing as coincidence...this is the Universes way of slapping you in face to get your attention.

SIGNS AND OMENS: AUGURIES AND FOREWARNINGS

Now that you have the vibrations of Para-X Power flowing through you, here are a few classic signs that have been recorded over the centuries by those who recognized the importance of these archetypical symbols. Many people still claim to be skeptical on the subject of signs, auguries, and forewarnings. However, those who are familiar with Para-X Powers will not deny that this phenomenon does exist.

The belief in signs and auguries has been cherished by mankind ever since the creation of the universe and this faculty is not confined to the human family alone. There are many animals that possess some awareness of these universal signs, sometimes to an extraordinary degree. The following are a few of the multifarious signs and auguries which admonish and forewarn mankind, at one time or another:

PARA-X POWERS

Should you be the subject of a deep depression of spirits, contrary to your usual constitutional buoyancy and liveliness, it is a sign that you are about to receive some agreeable intelligence.

If the crown of your head itches more than ordinary, you may expect to be advanced to a more honorable position in life. Should the hair on your head come off, when combing, in greater quantities than usual, it is a sign that you will soon be the subject of a severe attack of affliction.

If your right eyebrow should immoderately itch, be assured that you are going to look upon a pleasant sight – a long-absent friend, or a long-estranged, but now reconciled, lover.

Should your left eye-brow be visited with a tantalizing itching, it is a sign that you will soon look upon a painful sight – the corpse of a valued friend, or your lover walking with a favored rival.

A ringing in your right ear is an augury that you will shortly hear some pleasant news.

A ringing in your left ear is a sign that you will in a short time receive intelligence of a very unpleasant nature. When your left ear tingles some one is back-biting you.

A violent itching of the nose foretells trouble and sorrow to those who experience it.

An itching of the lips in a sign that some one is speaking disrespectfully of you.

When you are affected by an itching on the back of your neck, be assured that either yourself or some one nearly related to you is about to suffer a violent death.

An itching on the right shoulder signifies that you will shortly have a large legacy bequeathed to you.

When you feel an itching sensation on your left shoulder, be sure that you are about to bear a heavy burden of sorrow and trouble.

If your right elbow joint itches, you may expect shortly to hear some intelligence that will give you extreme pleasure.

PARA-X POWERS

Should you be annoyed with a violent itching on your left elbow joint, you may be sure that some vexatious disappointment will be experienced by you,

If you feel an itching on the palm of your right hand, you may expect soon to receive some money which you have been long expecting.

When the palm of your left hand itches, you may expect to be called upon to pay some money for a debt which you have not personally incurred.

An itching on the spine of your back is a sign that you will shortly be called upon to bear a heavy burden of sorrow and trouble.

An itching on your loins is an indication that you will soon receive an addition to your family, if married; if single, that you are on the eve of marriage.

When you are affected with an itching on the belly; expect to be invited to feast upon a choice collection of savory meats.

When either or both of your thighs itch, be assured that you are about to change your sleeping apartment.

If you have an itching sensation in your right knee, depend upon it that you will shortly undergo a remarkable and beneficial change in your previous course of life, and become religiously inclined.

If a similar sensation prevails in your right knee, you may expect to undergo a change in your deportment of an unfavorable nature.

An itching sensation on the shins foretells that you will be visited with a painful and long-continued affliction.

When your ankle-joints itch, be sure that you are about to be united to one whom you love, if single; if married, that your domestic comforts will be largely increased.

When the sole of your right foot itches, you may feel assured that you are about to undertake a journey from which you will derive much pleasure and enjoyment.

PARA-X POWERS

Should you experience a similar sensation on the sole of your left foot, you may expect to be called upon to take a journey of an unpleasant and melancholy nature.

If, in taking a walk, you should see a single magpie, it is a bad omen, especially if it should fly past you to the left hand; but if it should pass you to the right hand, the good will counterbalance the bad. Should you see two magpies together, expect to hear of something to your advantage – a proposal of marriage, if single; or a legacy of money bequeathed to you. Should the magpies fly past you together to your right hand, your own marriage, or the marriage of some one nearly related to you, will occur in a short time. The seeing of several magpies together is considered a very fortunate omen.

May is considered an unlucky month to marry in; therefore avoid doing so if possible. If you can catch a snail by the horns on the first of May, and throw it over your shoulders, you will be lucky throughout the year. If you place one on a slate on that day, it will describe by its turnings the initials of your future partner's name.

If a young man or young woman, on going up a flight of stairs, should stumble in the middle of the flight, it is a sign that his or her marriage will take place in a short time. If the stumbling should be near the top of the stairs, then his or her marriage will be immediately consummated.

If a young person, when seated at the tea-table, should observe one or more stalks of the tea-plant in the newly-poured-out cup, and if, on stirring the tea and holding the spoon in the middle of the liquid, the stalk or stalks should come close to the spoon handle, it is a token that he or she will be soon married.

When the house-dog is unusually restless, and howls dismally in the night-time, it is a sign that sickness and death are about to visit the family to whom the dog belongs.

When the wick of your candle shows a bright spark in the midst of the flame, it is a sign that a long-absent friend is about to visit you.

When the ribs of your fire-grate are more than usually covered with flukes of soot, it is a sign that a stranger is about to visit your habitation.

PARA-X POWERS

If a person stumbles when leaving his house at the beginning of a journey, or trips or stumbles more than once during the course of the journey, it is advisable to postpone it.

It is bad luck to sweep the kitchen floor after dark, and you are sweeping out good luck if you sweep dirt out the door.

If you burn beef bones by mistake it is a sign of much sorrow to come on account of poverty. To burn fish or poultry bones indicates that scandal will be spread about you.

To cross two forks accidentally is a sign that slander will be spread about you. To stir anything with a fork is to stir up misfortune. As well, crossing two table-knives by accident portends bad luck.

To be completely naked in your dream is a very lucky omen. If only your feet are bare, you will have many difficulties to overcome before you can reach your goal. Also, to dream of someone smoking a cigar indicates that money is on its way.

If you involuntarily make a rhyme, that is a lucky omen. Before speaking again, make a wish, and the chances are that it will come true.

It is a sign of good luck if you first see the new moon over your left shoulder, but of bad luck if you see it over your right. Should you have money in your pocket at the time of the new moon, you will be penniless before the moon is in the full.

To sneeze three times in rapid succession is considered by some to be a good omen.

It is a sure sign that your plans will meet with success if three bees alight on you at the same time.

If you find a coin, you should spit on it to bring good luck.

If the palm of the left hand itches you will be getting money; if the right palm itches, you will be losing/spending money.

A dog passing between a couple about to be married means ill fortune will befall the couple. However, being followed by a strange dog indicates good luck.

PARA-X POWERS

THE IMPORTANT SYMBOLS OF DREAMS

The symbolic meaning of dreams also plays an important role for the conveyance of useful information as directed by the Universe. These symbols can also be used in other Para-X activities such as reading the Para-Viewer.

This short list is by no means complete, nor should you think that the symbolic meanings are "set in stone." As we discussed earlier, your own personal symbolism is extremely important when considering the meanings of dreams, portents and omens. In order to understand the meanings of your dreams, you first have to become comfortable with being true to yourself and take a good look at what really makes you tick.

Abuse: There may be a dispute between you and the person with whom you do business. Take heed and be not slack in your attentions.

Accident: Personal afflictions may be inevitable. But you will remove soon from the trouble.

Accuse: This is a sign of great trouble. You will acquire riches by your own personal efforts.

Adultery: Troubles are approaching. Your prospects may be blasted. Despair will catch hold of you.

Advancement: A sign of success in all that you undertake.

Advocate: A dream that you are an advocate indicates that you will be prominent in future. You will win universal respect.

Affluence: This is not a favorable dream. It is indicatory of poverty.

Anger: The person with whom you are angry is your best friend.

Ass: All your great troubles, in spite of despairing circumstances, will end in ultimate success after much struggle and suffering.

Baby: If you are nursing a baby, it denotes sorrow and misfortune. If you see a baby that is sick, it means that somebody among your relatives will die.

PARA-X POWERS

Bachelor: Dreaming of a bachelor tells that you will shortly, meet with a friend.

Bankrupt: This is a dream of warning lest you should undertake something undesirable for you and also injurious to yourself. Be cautious in your transactions.

Battle: To dream of being in a battle means quarrel with neighbors or friends in a serious manner.

Beauty: To dream that you are beautiful indicates that you will become ugly with sickness and that you will become weak in body. Increasing beauty indicates death.

Birds: To see birds flying are very unlucky; it denotes sorrowful setback in circumstances. Poor persons may become better especially if they hear birds sing.

Birth: For unmarried women to dream of giving of birth to children is indicative of a new romance. For married women it indicates happy home life.

Blind: To dream of the blind is a sign that you will have no real friends.

Boat: To sail in a boat or ship on smooth waters is lucky. On rough waters, it is unlucky. To fall into water indicates great peril.

Books: To dream of books is an auspicious sign. Your future life will be very agreeable. Woman dreaming of books will get a son of eminent learning.

Bread: You will succeed in earthly business pursuits. Eating good bread indicates good health and long life. Burnt bread is a sign of funeral and so is bad.

Bride, Bridegroom: This dream is an unlucky one. It indicates sorrow and disappointment. You will mourn at the death of some relative.

Bugs: This indicates sure sickness. Many enemies are seeking to injure you.

Butter: Good dream. Joy and feasting. Sufferings terminate quickly.

PARA-X POWERS

Camel: Heavy burdens will come upon you. You will meet with heavy disasters. But you will bear with heroism.

Cat: This is a bad dream. This indicates treachery and fraud. Killing a cat indicates discovery of enemies.

Cattle: You will become rich and fortunate. Black and big-horned cattle indicate enemies of a violent nature.

Children: See Birth.

Clouds: Dark clouds indicate great sorrows that have to be passed through. But they will pass away if the clouds are moving or breaking away.

Corpse: Vision of a corpse indicates a hasty and imprudent engagement in which you will be unhappy.

Cow: Milking cow is a sign of riches. To be pursued by a cow indicates an overtaking enemy.

Crow: This indicates a sorrowful funeral ceremony.

Death: This indicates long life. But a sick person dreaming of death has the positive results.

Desert: Traveling across a desert shows the inevitability of a long and tedious journey. Accompaniment of sunshine indicates successful journey.

Devil: It is high time for you to mend yourself. Great evil may come to you. You must pursue virtue.

Dinner: If you are taking your dinner, it foretells great difficulties where you will be in want of meals. You will be uncomfortable. Enemies will try to injure your character. You should be careful about those whom you are confiding.

Disease: If a sick person dreams of disease it means recovery from the same. To young men it is a warning against evil company and intemperance.

Earthquake: This foretells that great trouble is going to come, loss in business, bereavement and separation. Family ties are broken by

114

death—quarrels in family and fear everywhere, heart breaking agony and disaster from all sides.

Eclipse: Hopes are eclipsed. Death is near. Enjoyment may be put an end to. There is no use of dotting on the wife, for life is coming to an end. The friend is a traitor. All expectations will bear no fruit.

Elephant: Good health, success, strength, prosperity, intelligence.

Embroidery: Those persons who love you are not true to their salt. They will deceive you.

Falling: If you dream you are falling but you are not frightened or harmed shows that you will meet with adversity but overcome it with ease. If the fall greatly frightens you then will you under go a major struggle in life. If you are injured in the fall you will lose many friends.

Famine: National prosperity and individual comfort. Much enjoyment. A dream of contrary.

Father: Father loves you. If the father is dead, it shows a sign of affliction.

Fields: Very great prosperity. To walk in green fields shows great happiness and wealth. However, scorched fields denote poverty.

Fighting: Quarrels in families. Misunderstanding among lovers, if not temporary separation. A bad dream for merchants, soldiers and sailors.

Fire: Health and great happiness, kind relations and warm friends.

Floods: Successful trade, safe voyage for traders. But to ordinary persons it indicates bad health and unfavorable circumstances.

Flying: Flying freely means that you feel really good about something in your life. You are likely very proud of an achievement at work or at home, and life is good. Flying in an airplane signifies that you feel proud of your accomplishments and that you expect and get recognition and support from those around you.

PARA-X POWERS

Flowers: Gathering beautiful flowers is an indication of prosperity. You will be very fortunate in all your undertakings.

Frogs: These creatures are not harmful. This dream therefore is not unfavorable. It denotes success.

Ghost: This is a very bad omen. Difficulties will be overwhelming. Terrible enemies will overpower you.

Giant: Great difficulty to be encountered. But meet it with boldness. Then it will vanish. This indicates that you will have an enemy of the most dreadful character.

Girl: Success, auspiciousness will come over you. Hopes will be fulfilled.

God: This is a rare dream which few people experience. Great success and elevation.

Grave: Some friend or relative will die. Recovery from illness doubtful.

Hanging: If you are hung, it is good to you. You will rise in society, and become wealthy.

Heaven: The remainder of your life will be spiritually happy, and your death will be peaceful.

Hell: There will be bodily suffering and also mental agony. Great suffering due to enemies and death of relatives, etc.

Home: To dream of home-life in early boyhood indicates good health and prosperity. Good sign of progress.

Husband: Your wish will not be granted. If you fall in love with another woman's husband, it indicates that you are growing vicious.

Ill: To dream that you are ill shows that you will have to fall a victim to some temptation, which, if you do not resist, will injure your character.

Injury: If you are injured by somebody else, it means that there are enemies to destroy you. Beware of them. Change of locality is desirable.

PARA-X POWERS

Itch: This is an unlucky dream. Denotes much difficulty and trouble. You will be unhappy.

Jail: If you dream that you are in jail it indicates that in life you will prosper. This is a dream of contrary.

Journey: This indicates that there will be a great change in conditions and circumstances. Good journey indicates good conditions and bad journey with troubles indicates a bad life.

King: To appear before a friendly king is a sign of great success and before a cruel king is very unfavorable.

Lamp: Very favorable dream. Very happy life. Family peaceful. This dream is always of good signs.

Learning: You will attain influence and respect. Good omen to dream that you are learning and acquiring knowledge.

Leprosy: To dream that you have leprosy always indicates a very great future misfortune. Perhaps you have committed some crime to be severely punished by law. You will have many enemies.

Light: To dream of lights is very good. It denotes riches and honor.

Limbs: Breakage of limbs indicates breakage of a marriage vow.

Lion: This dream indicates greatness, elevation and honor. You will become very important among men. You will become very powerful and happy.

Money: Receiving money in dream denotes earthly prosperity. Giving of it denotes ability to give money.

Mother: If you dream that you see your mother and converse with her, it indicates that you will have prosperity in life. To dream that you have lost your mother indicates her sickness.

Murder: To dream that you have murdered somebody denotes that you are going to become very bad and wretched, vicious and criminal.

Naked: Being naked in a dream is a very good symbol and shows that you are being asked to be yourself when it comes to the subject matter of the dream. The disturbing feeling usually associated with this type of dream, indicates the level of discomfort you would have in being yourself in the given situation.

Nectar: To drink nectar in dream indicates riches and prosperity. You will be beyond your expectations. You will marry a handsome person in high life and live in great state.

Nightmare: You are guided by foolish persons. Beware of such people.

Noises: To dream of hearing noises indicates quarrels in family and much misery in life.

Ocean: The state of life will be as the ocean is perceived to be in dream: calm and peaceful life when the ocean is calm and troublesome life when the ocean is stormy, etc.

Office: If you dream that you are turned out of the office it means that you will die or lose all property. This is a very bad dream for all people.

Owl: Denotes sickness and poverty, disgrace and sorrow. After dreaming of an owl, one need not have any hope of prosperity in life.

Palace: To live in a palace is a good omen. You will be elevated to a state of wealth and dignity.

Paradise: This is a very good dream. Hope of immortality and entrance into Paradise. Cessation of sorrows. Happy and healthy life.

Pigs: This indicates a mixture of good and bad luck. You will have great troubles but you will succeed. Many enemies are there, but there are some who will help you.

Prison: This is a dream of contrary. Indicates freedom and happiness.

Rain: This foretells trouble especially when it is heavy and boisterous. Gentle rain is a good dream indicating happy and calm life.

PARA-X POWERS

River: Rapid and flowing muddy river indicates great troubles and difficulties. But a river with calm glassy surface foretells happiness and love.

Ship: If you have a ship of your own sailing on the sea, it indicates advancement in riches. A ship that is tossed in the ocean and about to sink indicates disaster in life.

Singing: This is a dream of contrary. It indicates weeping and grief. Much suffering.

Snakes: You have sly and dangerous enemies who will injure your character and state of life.

Teeth: If you dream of having false teeth this indicates that you will have unexpected help on a problem. To dream of rotten teeth shows that you have been telling someone a lie or using your smooth words for getting your own way no matter what. If your teeth are rotten, crooked, and/or falling out this means that your lies are hurting someone very badly and that you will soon be found out. If you dream you have swallowed a tooth you will soon have too 'eat your words'. It becomes much easier to interpret this kind of dream if you think of teeth as representing words. When the dreamer is not the one with the bad teeth you will naturally have to watch out for someone lying to you.

Thunder: Great danger in life. Faithful friends will desert you. Thunder from a distance indicates that you will overcome troubles.

Volcano: Quarrels and disagreements in life.

Water: This indicates birth (of some person).

Wedding: This indicates that there is a funeral to be witnessed by you. To dream that you are married indicates that you will never marry. Marriage of sick persons indicates their death.

Young: To dream of young persons indicates enjoyment. If you are young, it indicates your sickness. You may die quickly.

119

PARA-X POWERS

11
ENERGIZE YOUR LIFE WITH PARA-X
CREATIVE POWER WORDS

FROM the inner planes of the Astral worlds there echoes a secret language...a secret language that any person can easily learn to understand and manipulate. You can learn how to hear this secret language of the Cosmos, and with the uttering of a few simple, yet infinitely powerful words or phrases, you can jump-start the creative energies of the Universe.

The ancient Mystic Sages of the Far-East used this power by meditating and uttering powerful mantras and chants given to them by the higher spiritual forces of the Astral worlds. Magicians of the Middle Ages would perform complicated and often time-consuming rites to draw the power out into the physical world of matter. In more recent times it has been called, by modern parapsychologists, the "alpha level" of the mind. You will be using a combination of all three to unleash Para-X energy into your life.

There is very little doubt that Para-X Creative Power Words, performed and carried out in the proper manner, possess the special quality of Universal Creative Force which can unite desire and latent abilities toward the attainment of a specific objective. You now have at your beck and call the ultimate occult power force, which has the potential to bring to you the key with which to alter your entire life forever.

HOW TO KEEP THE POWER FLOWING

To help ensure that every day for the rest of your mortal life is one filled with happiness, love, success, true friendship, money and good health, you should carry out a simple ritual that fills your life with Para-X Power. This ritual should be done daily for best results. The early morning and late at night is the best time to conduct this ritual. The Creative Energies will super-charge you to such an extent that you will begin to radiate outward from your auric field enough power to influence the thoughts and actions of others in your favor.

To start the flow of positive Para-X Power into every area of your life you should begin each new day by programming your mind with a series of positive chants, this in turn will help to stimulate your personal supply of Para-X Power toward the eventual manifestation of what you desire.

PARA-X POWERS

Put simply, a chant is a collection of specially selected words, describing a specific desire, which are uttered in a sing-song tone of voice. More often that not, the chant will rhyme, as this adds to the overall appeal and power of the chant. A chant, repeated ten to twenty times, until the very atmosphere appears to vibrate, generates potent occult power. Repetition is an important factor in generating, and releasing, genuine Para-X Power into the material world.

Repeat each of the following five Power Chants from ten to twenty times for maximum benefit in the quickest possible time and an absolute minimum of effort on your part. The positive Para-X Energy released through the repetition of the chants can then be united, and the power increased, with the power words as found in the longer, and more powerful, chants, spells, rituals, incantations, and invocations found in succeeding chapters. This in turn can help you to tune in to the Universal Creative Force.

"I am the most powerful and creative force in the Cosmos."

"I can perform miracles of health, wealth, and happiness."

"I know that Universal Energy is flowing through me every minute of my life."

"I do not accept unhappiness, illness, or poverty as my lot in life."

"I can achieve my every dream, goal, and desire."

Those positive chants will stir the Para-X Energies of the subconscious into dynamic and creative action. Your occult mind, your personal gateway to the Infinite, will then begin radiating out through your aura the powerful beams of externalized Para-X Energy which can draw to you whatever you truly desire out of life. Repetition of the above chants will cause them to be absorbed and assimilated into the mystic energies permeating your invisible occult mind. Many of you will, much to your delight, find that by doing nothing more than reciting the above chants will cause success and fulfillment to appear.

The power of externalized Para-X Power originates within your subconscious mind. This vast and invisible world is a power source filled with masses of spiritual rays of energy flowing into the material plain from the Astral worlds. When you fill your conscious mind with an all-powerful desire for a positive change in circumstances, these mystical inner energies are stirred, and stimulated into dynamic and creative action by thoughts formed, and crystallized by the strong emotional desire for changes in your life — and thus, the longed for results are produced.

/POWERFUL WORDS THAT RESONATE CREATIVE ENERGY

Every Para-Command that is sent to your subconscious during an extended period of time is duplicated, sooner or later, in tangible form in the outer objective world. Para-X Power responds to both positive and negative Para-Commands and external stimulation. You must learn to send your subconscious only the most positive and the most constructive of Para-Commands; rejecting forever any form of negative or self-defeating concept, if you ever hope to begin creating the bright and successful future you desire. A future built on Para-X Power.

Para-X Creative Power Words are sacred incantations. Every spoken word has a certain vibratory pattern. When sand grains are placed on an amplifying tray, actual wave patterns show up in the sand. The same thing can be demonstrated on an oscilloscope, which shows that each spoken word has a distinct amplitude and frequency.

Every word creates a distinct form in the Astral worlds. You can get a sense of this when you close your eyes and pay attention to the image that forms when you say different words (e.g., love, freedom, enemy, anger or happiness). Saying any word produces an actual physical vibration. Over time, if we know what the effect of that vibration is, then the word may come to have meaning associated with the effect of saying that vibration or word. This is one level of energy basis for words.

Another level is intent. If the actual physical vibration is coupled with a mental intention, the vibration then contains an additional mental component which influences the result of saying it. The sound is the carrier wave and the intent is overlaid upon the wave form. In either instance, the word is based upon energy.

Para-X Creative Power Words start a powerful vibration which corresponds to both a specific spiritual energy frequency and a state of consciousness in seed form. Over time, the energetic process begins to override all of the other smaller vibrations, which eventually become absorbed by the Power Word. After a length of time which varies from individual to individual, the great wave of the Power Word stills all other vibrations. Ultimately, the Power

PARA-X POWERS

Word produces a state where the organism vibrates at the rate completely in tune with the energy and spiritual state represented by and contained within the Power Word.

LET'S GET STARTED

Find a quiet room in which you will not be disturbed. You will need a straight-back chair on which to sit. Sit down, keep your spine erect, close your eyes and breathe slowly and deeply.

Now slowly repeat the desired Para-X Power Word, to be vibrated from the bottom of the lungs. Do this a total of fifty-two times, after which you can continue with your normal, daily routine.

While repeating the chosen Power Word keep the object of your desire firmly fixed within your mind. You are to repeat this entire exercise once a day, at a time convenient to you.

Continue until you receive your heart's desire, which should be obtained in a very short space of time, usually between seven and ten days.

NOTE: The chants herein are to be pronounced as they are spelt.

TIGRIS – Use this Power Word for overall success.

HUYUK – Use this Power Word to induce astral travel.

AEUNN – Use this Power Word to gain the love of a specific person or persons.

ENLIL – Use this Power Word for financial gain.

ZIGGURATS – Use this Power Word to heal a barren womb.

NIKIL – Use this Power Word to gain clairvoyant abilities (To see into the past and to foresee future events.)

LUGAL – Use this Power Word to detect lost objects.

URUK – Use this Power Word to win games where luck is involved such as pool, cards, bingo, horse racing, etc.

NINKILIM – Use this Power Word to remove any type of phobia.

UMMIA – Use this Power Word to rid any unwanted person from your life.

NANNAIYA – Use this Power Word to boost your sex drive.

NINGAL – Use this Power Word to heal both mental and physical ailments.

URNAMMU – Use this Power Word to induce lucidity within a dream (To become conscious within a dream.)

SHULGI – Use this Power Word to gain recognition in a chosen area of life.

LAZULI – Use this Power Word to boost your physical strength.

PARA-X POWERS

NIMKACY – Use this Power Word to gain telekinetic abilities (To move objects with the power of the mind.)

EUTRUSCAN – Use this Power Word for good visualisation abilities.

NINGRISU – Use this Power Word to strengthen your memory.

ZAGGRO – Use this Power Word to gain control over other people's thoughts.

LUGALLASAGESI – Use this Power Word to render any enemy harmless.

AKKAK – Use this Power Word to telepathically communicate with others.

ISHTAAR – Use this Power Word to improve your predictive abilities.

HAMMURABY – Use this Power Word to ensure a balanced state of mind.

CEREPLUX – Use this Power Word for general happiness.

TECCAS – Use this Power Word for psychic protection.

BITTATY – Use this Power Word to rid any addiction.

AKABIYAN – Use this Power Word to detect any enemies.

SHUSHU – Use this Power Word to gain mediumistic abilities (To communicate with departed spirits.)

GESHTYN – Use this Power Word to attract desired employment.

ATTRAHASIS – Use this Power Word for physical protection.

NEPHERAPHTI – Use this Power Word to overcome shyness.

AMMUNN – Use this Power Word to gain direct communion with God.

HELPHTAFMANNY – Use this Power Word to gain control over weather patterns.

ASHKKEENUTT – Use this Power Word to gain the respect of employers.

NETCHERGAMU – Use this Power Word to return any negative spell that has been cast against you back to the sender.

HALUGANCHY – Use this Power Word to gain invisibility from chosen persons.

PETTATRION – Use this Power Word to succeed in any legal dispute.

GEDBEGURU – Use this Power Word for meditating (This Power Word will still the mind.)

SOBEKTI – Use this Power Word to turn an enemy into a friend.

DJERGU – Use this Power Word to summon your guardian angel to appear before you (Only use when his services are absolutely necessary.)

GARNOPIC – Use this Power Word to induce levitation of the body.

PARA-X POWERS

VASTABA – Use this Power Word to gain clairaudient abilities (To hear spirit and angelic voices.)

ZAQGURRA – Use this Power Word to regress into past lives.

RARIT – Use this Power Word to help with artistic pursuits.

EKFAPHRATYNE – Use this Power Word to ensure protection of material objects such as house, any mode of transport, etc.

KATEMU – Use this Power Word for longevity (To increase the life-span of anything alive.)

TOWFAROT – Use this Power Word to bestow virility.

KILCOTH – Use this Power Word for success in any sponsoring activity.

MAATT – Use this Power Word to receive anything that is owed to you.

MEKERETRE – Use this Power Word to cure both male and female sterility.

PTHOPTECK – Use this Power Word to gain entry into the Akashic library.

BYBLOSTYIOUS – Use this Power Word for the ability to read the human aura.

PUABY – Use this Power Word to gain information about your future incarnation.

KHUFTU – Use this Power Word to prevent others from locking into your thoughts.

SWAFTIF – Use this Power Word to heal arthritis.

ZASSU – Use this Power Word to heal lung disorders such as asthma, bronchitis, etc.

ASUAN – Use this Power Word to heal bladder infections.

MINNAK – Use this Power Word to heal skin irritations such as eczema, measles, etc.

MYCENNO – Use this Power Word to heal headaches.

OMPEDMI – Use this Power Word to heal open wounds.

CHETHURUK – Use this Power Word to heal stomach complaints.

TALLNYET – Use this Power Word to heal influenza.

KEPURUTH – Use this Power Word to prevent hair-loss.

PSAZTHYRE – Use this Power Word to heal ear infections.

GALIPAL – Use this Power Word to prevent tooth decay. Use also to ease toothache.

ELYSIAD – Use this Power Word to heal torn muscles or tissues.

SHEEKAP – Use this Power Word to heal sexually transmitted diseases.

LIAZUSU – Use this Power Word to ease heart palpitations.

GANHAL – Use this Power Word to heal sore gums.

TYFHAIIA – Use this Power Word to overcome agoraphobia.

PARA-X POWERS

KURUCK – Use this Power Word to overcome claustrophobia.
PWANABAL – Use this Power Word to reverse any swelling.
PAPURJAMA – Use this Power Word to overcome general nervousness.
YANCKABAN – Use this Power Word to lower high blood pressure.

THE MOST POWERFUL SOUNDS IN THE UNIVERSE

The next list of Para-X Power Words are extremely powerful and energetic, they should not be taken lightly or misused. Their incorrect use can cause mental disorders, so please take care. These words are not spoken as normal speech but vibrated from the deep depths of the lungs, just as a baritone uses his voice.

The following Power Words each belong to individual universal vibrations, and if used correctly will make almost anything possible to achieve.

Phenomenal changes in consciousness will be produced by the Power Words; do not allow this to disturb you in any way. What this means is that auric energy is being released when this point is reached and it is a sure sign that things are moving in the right direction.

There is no need to construct any special temple to do the Power Words, just a room in which you feel comfortable and where you will not be disturbed. You will need a straight-backed chair, to support your spine, and a pair of earplugs as this will amplify the vibrations being worked with.

Sit down, close your eyes and slowly breathe in to the count of four, hold in for two, and exhale to the count of four. Do this exercise for about five minutes before re-starting any work with the Power Words.

After this exercise, place in your earplugs and sit quietly for about a few minutes, then when ready repeat the desired Power Word a total of fifty-two times.

The Para-X Power Words are to be pronounced as they are spelt unless otherwise stated. When this has been done sit quietly for another couple of minutes and think about what you desire.

The chosen ritual is to be done once a day until you succeed in getting what you want, which will take no longer than seven days to achieve.

BAEL – Use this Power Word for making yourself or an object invisible to other people.

PARA-X POWERS

AGARES – Use this Power Word to produce activity where there is stagnation.

VASSAGO – Use this Power Word for both psychic and physical protection.

SAMIGINA – Use this Power Word to stop any bad feeling between people; also use to correct any mistake.

MARBAS – Use this Power Word to pass examinations; good for all educational work.

VALEFOR – Use this Power Word for all inner workings such as pathworking.

AMON – Use this Power Word in any legal disputes.

BARBATOS – Use this Power Word to remove any spell cast upon you or friends.

PAIMON – Use this Power Word to remove anything unwanted.

BUER – Use this Power Word to heal any ailments.

GUSION – Use this Power Word to receive any secret information.

SITRI – Use this Power Word to gain sex drive, or to make others gain sex drive.

BELETH – Use this Power Word to gain the love of someone special.

LERAJE – Use this Power Word to cure headaches or for a general pick-me-up.

ELIGOS – Use this Power Word for inner strength and positive thoughts.

ZEPAR – Use this Power Word to ensure conception; use for all fertility rites.

BOTIS – Use this Power Word for tranquility and general happiness.

BATHIN – Use this Power Word to separate the consciousness from the physical and project onto the astral plane. Use also to dream lucidly.

SALLOS – Use this Power Word to become 'at-one' with all creation.

PURSON – Use this Power Word for successful interviews, blind dates and for successful business advertising.

MARAX – Use this Power Word for clear and mature thinking.

IPOS – Use this Power Word to overcome any kind of phobia.

AIM – Use this Power Word for easier breathing. Excellent for asthma.

NABERIOUS – Use this Power Word for communication with discarnate friends, spirits and angels.

GLASYALABOLAS – Use this Power Word to dissolve any unwanted situation.

PARA-X POWERS

BUNE – Use this Power Word to gain large amounts of money.

RONOVE – Use this Power Word for general stability.

BERITH – Use this Power Word to gain recognition.

ASTAROTH – Use this Power Word for overall success.

FORNEUS – Use this Power Word to gain fame in a chosen career.

FORAS – Use this Power Word for good health and a long life.

ASMODAY – Use this Power Word to abstain spirit help and guidance.

GAAP – Use this Power Word to keep secrets hidden from others.

FURFUR – Use this Power Word to keep tempers cool; good for calmness.

MARCHOSIAS – Use this Power Word to summon your personal guardian angel.

STOLAS – Use this Power Word for practicality.

PHENEX – Use this Power Word for general happiness and tranquility.

HALPHAS – Use this Power Word for self-esteem and moral strength.

MALPHAS – Use this Power Word when feeling down (It will pick you up.)

RAUM – Use this Power Word to receive visions of lost objects, and where they will be.

FOCALOR – Use this Power Word to return negative spells back to their sender.

VEPAR – Use this Power Word to prevent storms from breaking down hot, settled, summer weather.

SABNOCK – Use this Power Word to send telepathic messages.

SHAX – Use this Power Word to keep enemies at bay. A protection Power Word.

VINE – Use this Power Word if you desire to formulate your own rituals and spells. It will enhance creativity.

BIFRONS – Use this Power Word to strengthen your willpower.

VUAL – Use this Power Word to gain psychometric abilities (The reading and interpreting of vibrations within an object.)

HAAGENTI – Use this Power Word to transform your life from old habits to new adventures.

CROCELL – Use this Power Word for general happiness.

FURCAS – Use this Power Word to gain clairvoyant abilities to divine the future.

BALAM – Use this Power Word to communicate with the spiritual 'masters'.

ALLOCES – Use this Power Word to gain wisdom directly from the spirit-source.

PARA-X POWERS

CAMIO – Use this Power Word for good intuitive abilities.

MURMUR – Use this Power Word to induce total calmness in both body and mind.

OROBAS – Use this Power Word to induce ethereal projection (To project the consciousness from
the physical body and travel anywhere at will within the physical plane.)

GREMORY – Use this Power Word to see with clairvoyant sight.

OSE – Use this Power Word to gain telekinetic abilities (To be able to move objects with the mind.)

AMY – Use this Power Word to gain the ability to interpret the message of dreams.

ORIAS – Use this Power Word to control weather patterns as you choose.

VAPULA – Use this Power Word to produce divine sounds within your place of abode (You will hear divine messages.)

ZAGAN – Use this Power Word to gain mediumship abilities.

VALAC – Use this Power Word to gain entry into the Elysian Fields. (The land where the gods of Ancient Greece reside.)

ANDRAS – Use this Power Word to release negative 'thoughts' from your mind.

HAURES – Use this Power Word for creative abilities, such as painting, writing, playing instruments, etc.

ANDREALPHUS – Use this Power Word to summon the salamander spirits to work under your command. (Do not pronounce the second letter 'A' in this Power Word.)

CIMEJES – Use this Power Word to insure against theft and fire.

AMDUSIAS – Use this Power Word to gain the ability to see the human aura.

BELIAL – Use this Power Word to raise 'kundalini' and move the spirit outside the physical body to travel at will. (The spirit is pure, so this exercise is not the same as projection of the etheric body.)

DECARABIA – Use this Power Word to dissolve 'negative' thought patterns.

SEERE – Use this Power Word to obtain information on who you were in previous lives.

DANTALION – Use this Power Word to gain visions of the 'hereafter' and loved ones who have passed on.

ANDROMALIUS – Use this Power Word for deep meditation work.

PARA-X POWERS

POWER WORDS FOR ATTRACTING LOVE

Here are a special group of Power Words called "Mantras," to be used specifically for attracting a romantic partner. These Power Words come to us from the book: *What's Your Dosha, Baby? Discover the Vedic Way for Compatibility in Life and Love*, by Lissa Coffey.

In any endeavor, the results that we achieve are the result of the quality of our intentions. We need to begin with a clear understanding of exactly what it is that we are going for. In the West, we tend to base our criteria for relationships on superficial values. For example, men seem to want women who look good, and women seem to want men with money. Sure, we could look down the list and find a sense of humor, a love of family, and all those good things. But are we really defining what would satisfy the soul? The Vedic texts have a different way of placing value on a relationship, one that is meant to help us grow spiritually as individuals and as couples.

Using a mantra helps to both awaken, and to bring into balance, the Shiva and Shakti within us. At the same time, the mantra strengthens our power of attraction, it makes us like a magnet, and people are drawn to us. This is another reason why we need to have a clear understanding of what we want. Our intention can't merely be for "some rich guy" or "some beautiful girl."

When we are seeking our life partner, we are seeking someone who will respect and honor our energies, someone who will give their energy for our good in return. And we are seeking truth.

From truth comes all those other great things that make a relationship last, including trust. So it is important to be clear not only in the words we say, but in the thoughts we think as well.

Here is the mantra to use when a woman seeks a man:

Sat Patim Dehi

This is pronounced: Saht Pahteem Dayhee.

It translates to "Please bring me a man of truth and goodness."

PARA-X POWERS

Here is the mantra to use when a man seeks a woman:

Patneem Manoramam Dehi

This is pronounced: Pahtneem Mahnoramahm Dayhee.

It translates to "Please bring me a woman of truth and beauty."

What determines the effectiveness of the mantra the most is how much devotion and concentration is behind it. Like everything else in life, we'll get out of it what we put into it. If you are serious about your search, and have strong intention, you will want to put effort into this task.

While you can repeat your mantra anywhere, anytime of day, it is nice to set some special time aside just for the ritual of the mantra. Before beginning your practice, wash your hands, as this symbolizes purity.

Find a comfortable place where you can be quiet and undisturbed for awhile. If it will help you get in the mood, you may choose to sit facing the east, to light a candle, and/or to sit in a cross-legged position. Close your eyes, and concentrate on each syllable of the mantra. Mantras may be repeated either silently or out loud. Continue repeating the mantra over and over again. The repetition will bring you a deep sense of peace and joy. When you feel you are done, sit quietly

for a moment, and give thanks to the Siddhas, the sages of Ancient India, for their wisdom and generosity in passing these mantras on for us to use. Then slowly open your eyes, take a few breaths, and go on with your usual activity.

12
SECRETS OF THE HUMAN AURA

THERE has been a lot written about the human aura over the years and the subject remains to this day extremely controversial. Because learning how to see the human aura can be very difficult, many people do not even attempt to learn how to do it. This is unfortunate because auras can reveal a lot a lot about a person that can be used to your benefit.

A person's aura can show you if they are healthy or sick; if they are lying to you or telling the truth; you can even tell if someone if in love with you through their aura. As well, those seeking a little "inside" information in making money or trying to succeed in business can definitely use the ability to see the aura to their benefit.

Your ability to use your Para-X Powers for successful viewing of the human aura can really help you get ahead in life. So, do not dismiss learning to see the aura as "being too hard" to be worth the effort.

KIRLIAN PHOTOGRAPHY AND THE HUMAN AURA

Even though experts in Para-X Powers have been teaching about the human aura for centuries, there was little scientific evidence that such an energy field surrounding the human body actually existed. However, in 1939 a Russian engineer named Semyon Kirlian, was busy repairing an electro-therapy machine in the research laboratory of his town in the Ukraine when he made an interesting discovery.

Kirlian got a little careless and his hand strayed near to a live electrode when he received a shock and also witnessed a flash of light. He was struck with the curious idea that it would be interesting to place a piece of light sensitive material in front of this flash of light.

He placed some suitable material between his hand and his equipment and essentially photographed the result. The developed image was quite extraordinary in that it showed streamer like emanations coming from his fingertips, each emanation had its own unique radiation pattern.

Fascinated by his findings, Kirlian began to dedicate much of his time to a home-based investigation of the subject. Over the next 40 years his high voltage photography produces much scientific speculation and even claims that he had proved the existence of the "astral body."

Others replicated his results and made new discoveries. The English researcher George de la Warr found that a lattice-like formation of electromagnetic force fields surrounded the body up to some distance. It had peaks of as much as 70 milli-volts, although fluctuating, usually with the emotional state of the subject.

Kirlian found evidence that illness also had an effect on the energy field, when taking a picture of himself just before a very virulent attack of influenza hardly any image resulted from his photos. This finding was reinforced by a blind test initiated by a respected head of a scientific investigative unit, two leaves were photographed by the method, yet one lacked the characteristic energy patterns. It was later revealed that the leaf was from a plant that had contracted a serious disease.

Other interesting findings were made when parts of leaves were imaged, as these produces pictures showing ghostly images of complete leaves in outline at least, as though the remainder retained the energy field make-up of the original whole unit. Rather like the phantom limb syndrome felt by amputees, in which sensations or irritations are felt in parts of the body that have been removed some time before.

Although many have over the years attributed the findings of Kirlian photography to the existence of an Astral body, Kirlian never did so himself. Indeed many mystics argue that the images do not represent anything like the subtlety and complex imagery that can be seen in the human aura by psychics. A scientific investigation of the human aura is incredibly difficult as it is so inherently personal and therefore not easily analysed or quantified by an objective methodology.

At least we have taken a first step in verifying the reality of the human aura. A lot of research still needs to be done in this field. Until that time, we still have the meticulous research done by such early Para-X Power researchers as Swami Panchadasi who was very successful in his studies and his abilities to train others on how to look for the human aura.

THE MYSTERY OF THE HUMAN AURA

What is the human aura? This question is frequently asked the student of occultism by someone who has heard the term but who is unfamiliar with its meaning. Simple as the question may seem, it is by no means easy to answer it plainly and clearly in a few words unless the hearer already has a general acquaintance with the subject of occult science. Let us commence at the beginning and consider the question from the point of view of the person who has just heard the term for the first time.

The dictionaries define the word aura as: "Any subtle, invisible emanation or exhalation." The English authorities, as a rule, attribute the origin of the word to a Latin term meaning "air," but the Hindu authorities insist that it had its origin in the Sanskrit root at, meaning the spoke of a wheel, the significance being perceived when we remember the fact that the human aura radiates from the body of the individual in a manner similar to the radiation of the spokes of a wheel from the hub thereof. The Sanskrit origin of the term is the one preferred by occultists, although it will be seen that the idea of an aerial emanation, indicated by the Latin root, is not foreign to the real significance of the term.

Be the real origin of the term what it may, the idea of the human aura is one upon which all occultists are in full agreement and harmony, and the mention of which is found in all works upon the general subject of occultism. So we shall begin by a consideration of the main conception thereof, as held by all advanced occultists, ancient and modern, omitting little points of theoretical variance between the different schools.

Briefly, then, the human aura may be described as a fine, ethereal radiation or emanation surrounding each and every living human being. It extends from two to three feet, in all directions, from the body. It assumes an oval shape, a great egg-shaped nebula surrounding the body on all sides. This aura is sometimes referred to, in ordinary terms, as the "psychic atmosphere" of a person, or as his "magnetic atmosphere."

This atmosphere or aura is apparent to a large percentage of persons in the sense of the psychic awareness generally called "feeling," though the term is not a clear one. The majority of persons are more or less aware of that subtle something about the personality of others which can be sensed or felt in a clear though unusual way when the other persons are near by, even though they may be out of the range of the vision.

Being outside of the ordinary range of the five senses, we are apt to feel that there is something queer or uncanny about these feelings of projected personality. But every person, deep in his heart, knows them to be realities and admits their effect upon his impressions regarding the persons from whom they emanate. Even small children, infants even, perceive this influence and respond to it in the matter of likes and dislikes.

But human testimony regarding the existence and character of the human aura does not stop with the reports of the psychic senses to which we have just referred. There are many individuals of the race, a far greater percentage than is generally imagined, who have the gift of psychic sight more or less developed. Many persons have quite a well-developed power of this kind, who do not mention it to their acquaintances for fear of ridicule, or of being thought "weird."

In addition to these persons, there are here and there to be found well-developed, clear-sighted or truly clairvoyant persons whose powers of psychic perception are as highly developed as are the ordinary senses of the average individual. And the reports of these persons, far apart in time and space though they may be, have always agreed on the main points of psychic phenomena, particularly in regards to the human aura.

To the highly developed clairvoyant vision, every human being is seen as surrounded by the egg-shaped aura of two or three feet in depth, more dense and thick in the portion nearest the body, and then gradually becoming more tenuous, thin and indistinct as the distance from the body is increased. By the psychic perception, the aura is seen as a luminous cloud – a phosphorescent flame – deep and dense around the center and then gradually shading into indistinctness toward the edges. As a matter of fact, as all developed occultists know, the aura really extends very much farther than even the best clairvoyant vision can perceive it, and its psychic influence is perceptible at quite a distance in many cases. In this respect it is like any flame on the physical plane, it gradually fades into indistinctness, its rays persisting far beyond the reach of the vision, as may be proved by means of chemical apparatus, etc.

To the highly developed clairvoyant vision, the human aura is seen to be composed of all the colors of the spectrum, the combinations of colors differing in various persons, and constantly shifting in the case of every person. These colors reflect the mental (particularly the emotional) states of the person in whose aura they are manifested.

Each mental state has its own particular combination formed from the few elementary colors which represent the elementary mental conditions. As the mind is ever shifting and changing its states, it follows that there will ever be a corresponding series of shifting changes in the colors of the human aura.

The shades and colors of the aura present an ever changing kaleidoscopic spectacle of wonderful beauty and most interesting character. The trained occultist is able to read the character of any person, as well as the nature of his passing thoughts and feelings, by simply studying the shifting colors of his aura. To the developed occultist, the mind and character become as an open book, to be studied carefully and intelligently.

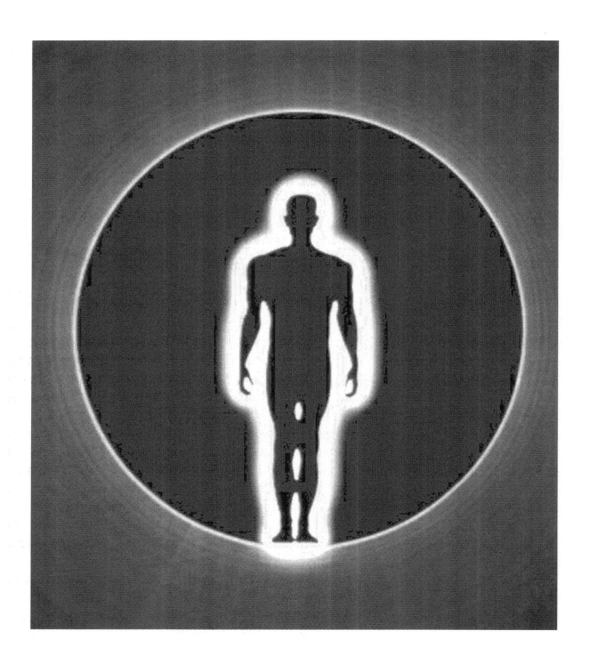

The human aura is a fine, ethereal radiation or emanation surrounding every living human being. It extends from two to three feet, in all directions, from the body. This aura is sometimes referred to, in ordinary terms, as the "psychic atmosphere" of a person, or as his "magnetic atmosphere."

PARA-X POWERS

Even the student of occultism who has not been able to develop the clairvoyant vision to such a high degree is soon able to develop the sense of psychic perception whereby he is able to at least "feel" the vibrations of the aura, though he may not see the colors, and thus be able to interpret the mental states which have caused them. The principle is, of course, the same, as the colors are but the outward appearance of the vibrations themselves, just as the ordinary colors on the physical plane are merely the outward manifestation of vibration of matter.

But it must not be supposed that the human aura is always perceived in the appearance of a luminous cloud of ever-changing color. When we say that such is its characteristic appearance, we mean it in the same sense that we describe the ocean as a calm, deep body of greenish waters. We know, however, that at times the ocean presents no such appearance, but instead is seen as rising in great mountainous waves, white capped and threatening the tiny vessels of men with its power. Or again we may define the word flame in the sense of a steady bright stream of burning gas, whereas we know only too well that the word also indicates the great hot tongues of fiery force that stream out from the windows of a burning building and lick to destruction all with which it comes in contact.

So it is with the human aura. At times it may be seen as a beautiful, calm, luminous atmosphere, presenting the appearance of a great opal under the rays of the sun. Again, it blazes like the flames of a great furnace, shooting forth great tongues of fire in this direction and that, rising and falling in great waves of emotional excitement or passion, or perhaps whirling like a great fiery maelstrom toward its center, or swirling in an outward movement away from its center.

Again, it may be seen as projecting from its depths smaller bodies or centers of mental vibration, which like sparks from a furnace, detach themselves from the parent flame and travel far away in other directions – these are the projected thought forms of which all occultists are fond of speaking and which make plain many strange psychic occurrences.

So, it will be seen, the human aura is a very important and interesting phase of the personality of every individual. The psychic phase of man is as much the man himself as is the physical phase – the complete man being made up of the two phases. Man invisible is as much the real man as is man visible. As the finer forms of nature are always the most powerful, so is the psychic man more potent than the physical man.

In this chapter, I speak of the human aura and its colors as being perceived by astral or clairvoyant vision as produced with the help of Para-X Power, for this is the way in which it is perceived and studied by the occultist. The occult teaching is that, in the evolution of the race, this astral vision will eventually become the common property of every human being; it so exists even now, and needs only development to perfect it.

But modern physical science is today offering corroborative proof (though the same is not needed by the occultist who has the astral vision) to the general public, of the existence of the human aura. Leading authorities all over the world have reported the discovery of a nebulous, hazy, radioactive energy or substance around the body of human beings. In short, they now claim that every human being is radioactive, and that the auric radiation may be registered and perceived by means of a screen composed of certain fluorescent material interposed between the eye of the observer and the person observed.

This aura is called by them the "human atmosphere" and is classified by them as similar to the radiations of other radioactive substances, radium, for instance. They have failed to discover color in this atmosphere, however, and know nothing, apparently, of the relation between auric colors and mental and emotional states, which are so familiar to every advanced occultist.

This fact is mentioned merely as a matter of general interest and information to the student, and not as indicating, even in the slightest degree, any idea on my part that the old occult teaching and the observed phenomena accompanying the same regarding the human aura require any proof or backing up on the part of material scientists.

THE PRANA-AURA

Many writers on the subject of the human aura content themselves with a description of the colors of the mental or emotional aura, and omit almost any reference whatsoever to the basic substance or power of the aura. This is like the play of Hamlet with the character of Hamlet omitted, for, unless we understand something concerning the fundamental substance of which the aura is composed, we cannot expect to arrive at a clear understanding of the phenomena which arise from and by reason of the existence of this fundamental substance. We might as well expect a student to understand the principles of color without having been made acquainted with the principles of light.

The fundamental substance of which the human aura is composed is none other than that wonderful principle of nature of which one reads so much in all occult writings, which has been called by many names, but which is perhaps best known under the Sanskrit term prana, but which may be thought of as vital essence, life power, etc.

It is not necessary in this book to go into the general consideration of the nature and character of prana. It is sufficient for us to consider it in its manifestation of vital force, life essence, etc. In its broadest sense, prana really is the principle of energy in nature, but in its relation to living forms it is the vital force which lies at the very basis of manifested Life. It exists in all forms of living things, from the smallest microscopic form up to living creatures on higher planes, as much higher than man as man is higher than the simple microscopic life forms. It permeates them all and renders possible all life activity and functioning.

Prana is not the mind or the soul, but is rather the force or energy through which the soul manifests activity, and the mind manifests thought. It is the steam that runs the physical and mental machinery of life. It is the substance of the human aura, and the colors of mental states are manifested in that substance, just as the colors of chemical bodies are manifested in the substance of water. But prana is not material substance--being the underlying substance of energy or force in nature.

While it is true, as we have seen, that all auras are composed of the substance of prana, it is likewise true that there is a simple and elementary form of auric substance to which occultists have given the simple name of the prana-aura in order to distinguish it from the more complex forms and phases of the human aura. The simplicity of the character of the prana-aura causes it to be more readily sensed or perceived than is possible in the case of the more complex phases or forms of the aura. For whereas it is only the more sensitive organisms that can distinguish the finer vibrations of the mental and emotional aura, and only the clairvoyant sight which can discern its presence by its colors, almost any person, by a little careful experimenting, may become aware of the presence of the prana-aura, not only in the way of "feeling" it, but in many cases of actually seeing it with the ordinary vision rightly directed.

That which is known as the prana-aura is of course the most simple form or phase of the human aura. It is the form or phase which is more closely bound up with the physical body, and is less concerned with the mental states. This fact has caused some writers to speak of it as the "health aura," or "physical aura," both of which terms are fittingly applied as we shall see, although we prefer the simpler term we have used here, the prana-aura. For the prana-aura does show the state of the health of the individual radiating it and it also really contains physical power and magnetism which may be and is imparted to others.

PARA-X POWERS

The basic prana-aura is practically colorless; that is to say, it is about the color of the clearest water or a very clear diamond. By the clairvoyant vision it is seen to be streaked or marked by very minute, bristle-like lines radiating outward from the physical body of the individual in a manner very like "the quills upon the fretful porcupine," as Shakespeare puts it. In the case of excellent physical health, these bristle-like streaks are stiff and brittle-looking, whereas, check punctuation of whereas if the general health of the person be deficient these bristle-like radiations seem to be more or less tangled, twisted or curly, and in some cases present a drooping appearance, and in extreme cases present the appearance of soft, limp fur.

It may interest the student to know that minute particles of this prana-aura, or vital magnetism, is sloughed off the body in connection with physical exhalations such as scent, etc., and remain in existence for some time after the person has passed from the particular place at which they were cast off. In fact, as all occultists know, it is these particles of the prana-aura which serve to give vitality to the "scent" of living creatures, which enables dogs and other animals to trace up the track of the person or animal for a long time after the person has passed. It is not alone the physical odor, which must be very slight as you will see upon a moment's consideration. It is really the presence of the particles of the prana-aura which enables the dog to distinguish the traces of one person among that of thousands of others, and the feat is as much psychical as physical.

Another peculiarity of the prana-aura is that it is filled with a multitude of extremely minute sparkling particles, resembling fiery electric sparks, (as photographed with Kirlian photography) which are in constant motion. These sparks, which are visible to persons of only slightly developed psychic power, impart a vibratory motion to the prana-aura which under certain conditions is plainly visible to the average person. This vibratory movement is akin to the movement of heated air arising from a hot stove, or from the heated earth on a mid-summer day.

If the student will close his eyes partially until he peers out from narrowed lids, and then will closely observe some very healthy person sitting in a dim light, he may perceive this undulating, pulsing vibration extending an inch or two from the surface of the body. It requires some little knack to recognize these vibrations, but a little practice will often give one the key; and after the first recognition, the matter becomes easy.

Again, in the case of persons of active brains, one may perceive this pulsating prana-aura around the head of the person, particularly when he is engaged in concentrated active thought. A little practice will enable almost anyone to perceive faintly the dim outlines of the prana-aura around his own fingers and hand by placing his hand against a black background, in a dim light, and then gazing at it with narrowed eyelids, squinting if necessary. Under these circumstances, after a little practice, one will be apt to perceive a tiny outlined aura, or radiation, or halo of pale yellowish light surrounding the hand.

By extending the fingers fan shape you will perceive that each finger is showing its own little outlined prana-aura. The stronger the vital force, the plainer will be the perception of the phenomenon. Often the prana-aura, in these experiments, will appear like the semi-luminous radiance surrounding a candle flame or gas light. Under the best conditions, the radiation will assume an almost phosphorescent appearance. Remember, this is simply a matter of trained ordinary sight, not clairvoyant vision.

This prana-aura is identical with human magnetism, which is employed in ordinary magnetic healing. That is to say it is the outer manifestation of the wonderful pranic force. It is felt when you shake hands or otherwise come in close physical contact with a strongly magnetic person. On the other hand it is what the weakly, human vampire-like persons unconsciously, or consciously, try to draw off from strong persons, if the latter allow them so to do from want of knowledge of self protection.

Who has not met persons of this kind, who seem to sap one's very life force away from him? Remember, then, that the prana-aura is the aura or radiation of life force, or vital power, which is the steam of your living activity, physical and mental. It is the pouring out of the vital "steam" which is running your vital machinery. Its presence indicates life--its absence lifelessness.

THE ASTRAL COLORS

The term astral, so frequently employed by all occultists, is difficult to explain or define except to those who have pursued a regular course of study in occult science. For the purpose of the present consideration, it is enough to say that over and above the ordinary physical sense plane there is another and more subtle plane, known as the astral plane. Every human being possesses the innate and inherent faculty of sensing the things of this astral plane, by means of an extension or enlargement of the powers of the ordinary senses, so to speak.

But in the majority of persons in the present stage of development, these astral senses are lying dormant, and only here and there do we find individuals who are able to sense on the astral plane, although in the course of evolution the entire race will be able to do so, of course. The colors of the human aura, which arise from the various mental and emotional states, belong to the phenomena of the astral plane and hence bear the name of "the astral colors."

Belonging to the astral plane, and not to the ordinary physical plane, they are perceived only by the senses functioning on the astral plane, and are invisible to the ordinary physical plane sight. But to those who have developed the astral sight, or clairvoyance, these colors are as real as are the ordinary colors to the average person, and their phenomena have been as carefully recorded by occult science as have the physical plane colors by physical science.

The fact that to the ordinary physical senses they are invisible does not render them any the less real. Remember, in this connection, that to the blind man our physical colors do not exist. And, for that matter, the ordinary colors do not exist to "color blind" persons. The ordinary physical plane person is simply "color blind" to the astral colors – that's all.

On the astral plane each shade of mental or emotional state has its corresponding astral color, the latter manifesting when the form appears. It follows then, of course, that when once the occultist has the key to this color correspondence, and thus is able to perceive the astral colors by means of his astral vision, he also is able to read the mental and emotional states of any person within the range of his vision, as easily as you are now reading the printed words of this book.

Before proceeding to a consideration of the list of astral colors in the human aura, I wish to call your attention to a slight variation in the case of the prana-aura. I have stated that the prana-aura is colorless, like a diamond or clear water. This is true in the average case, but in the case of a person of very strong physical vitality or virility, the prana-aura takes on, at times, a faint warm pink tinge, which is really a reflection from the red astral color, the meaning of which color you shall now learn.

Like their physical plane counterparts, all the astral colors are formed from three primary colors, namely: (1) red; (2) blue; and (3) yellow. From these three primary colors, all other colors are formed. Following the primary colors, we find what are known as the secondary colors, namely: (1) green, derived from a combination of yellow and blue; (2) orange, formed from a combination of yellow and red; and (3) purple, formed from a combination of red and blue. Further combinations produce the other colors, as for instance, green and purple form olive; orange and purple form russet; green and orange form citrine.

PARA-X POWERS

Black is called an absence of color, while white is really a harmonious blending of all colors, strange as this may appear to one who has not studied the subject. The blending of the primary colors in varied proportions produce what is known as the "hues" of color. Adding white to the hues, we obtain "tints," while mixing black produces "shades." Strictly speaking, black and white are known as "neutral" colors.

Now for the meaning of the astral colors — that is, the explanation of the mental or emotional state represented by each. I ask that the student familiarize himself with the meaning of the primary colors and their combinations. A clear understanding of the key of the astral colors is often an aid in the development of astral sight.

KEY TO THE ASTRAL COLORS

Red: Red represents the physical phase of mentality. That is to say, it stands for that part of the mental activities which are concerned with physical life. It is manifested by the vitality of the body, and in other hues, tints and shades, is manifested by passions, anger, physical cravings, etc. I shall describe the various forms of red manifestation a little later on.

Blue: Blue represents the religious, or spiritual, phase of mentality. That is to say, it stands for that part of the mental activities which are concerned with high ideals, altruism, devotion, reverence, veneration, etc. It is manifested, in its various hues, tints and shades, by all forms of religious feeling and emotion, high and low, as we shall see as we proceed.

Yellow: Yellow represents the intellectual phase of mentality. That is to say, it stands for that part of the mental activities which are concerned with reasoning, analysis, judgment, logical processes, induction, deduction, synthesis, etc. In its various hues, tints and shades, it is manifested by the various forms of intellectual activity, high and low, as we shall see as we proceed.

White: White stands for what occultists know as Pure Spirit, which is a very different thing from the religious emotion of "spirituality," and which really is the essence of the All that really is. Pure Spirit is the positive pole of Being. We shall see the part played by it in the astral colors, as we proceed.

143

PARA-X POWERS

Black: Black stands for the negative pole of Being--the very negation of Pure Spirit, and opposing it in every way. We shall see the part played by it in the astral colors as we proceed.

The various combinations of the three astral primary colors are formed in connection with black and white as well as by the blending of the three themselves. These combinations, of course, result from the shades of mental and emotional activity manifested by the individuality, of which they are the reflection and the key.

The combinations and blending of the astral colors, however, are numberless, and present an almost infinite variety. Not only is the blending caused by the mixing of the colors themselves, in connection with black and white, but in many cases the body of one color is found to be streaked, striped, dotted or clouded by other colors. At times there is perceived the mixture of two antagonistic color streams fighting against each other before blending. Again we see the effect of one color neutralizing another.

In some cases great black clouds obscure the bright colors beneath and then darken the fierce glow of color, just as is often witnessed in the case of a physical conflagration. Again, we find great flashes of bright yellow or red flaring across the field of the aura, showing agitation or the conflict of intellect and passion.

The average student who has not developed the astral vision is inclined to imagine that the astral colors in the human aura present the appearance of an egg-shaped rainbow or spectrum, or something of that sort. But this is a great mistake. In the first place, the astral colors are seldom at rest, for all mental and emotional activity is the result of vibration, change and rhythmic motion. Consequently, the colors of the aura present a kaleidoscopic appearance of constant change of color, shape and grouping – a great electrical display, so to speak, constantly shifting, changing and blending.

Great tongues of flame-like emanations project themselves beyond the border of the aura under strong feeling or excitement, and great vibratory whirls and swirls are manifested. The sight is most fascinating, although somewhat terrifying at first. Nature is wise in bestowing the gift of astral vision only gradually and by almost imperceptible stages of advance. There are many unpleasant, as well as pleasant, sights on the astral plane.

Remembering always the significance of the three primary colors on the astral plane, let us consider the meaning of the combinations, shades, hues and tints of these colors.

The Red Group: In this group of astral colors seen in the human aura we find strongly in evidence the clear bright red shade, similar to that of fresh, pure arterial blood as it leaves the

144

heart, filled with pure material freshly oxygenated. This shade in the aura indicates health, life-force, vigor, virility, etc., in pure and untainted form. The aura of a healthy, strong child shows this shade of color very plainly and strongly.

Strong, pure natural emotions, such as friendship, love of companionship, love of physical exercise, healthy clean sports, etc., are manifested by a clear, clean shade of red. When these feelings become tainted with selfishness, low motives, etc., the shade grows darker and duller. Love of low companionship, unclean sports or selfish games, etc., produce an unpleasant, muddy red shade.

A shade of red very near to crimson is the astral color of love, but the tint and shade vary greatly according to the nature of this form of emotional feeling. A very high form of love, which seeks the good of the loved one, rather than the satisfaction of oneself, manifests as a beautiful rose tint, one of the most pleasing of the astral tints, by the way. Descending in the scale, we find the crimson shade becoming darker and duller, until we descend to the plane of impure, sensual, coarse passion, which is manifested by an ugly, dull, muddy crimson of a repulsive appearance, suggesting blood mixed with dirty earth or barnyard soil.

A peculiar series of red shades are those manifesting anger in its various forms, from the vivid scarlet flashes of anger color, arising from what may be called "righteous indignation," down the scale to the ugly flashes of deep, dull red, betokening rage and uncontrolled passion. The red of anger generally shows itself in flashes, or great leaping flames, often accompanied by a black background, in the case of malicious hate, or by a dirty, greenish background when the rage arises from jealousy or envy. The color of avarice is a very ugly combination of dull, dark red and a dirty ugly green.

If persons could see their own astral colors accompanying these undesirable mental states, the sight would perhaps so disgust them with such states as to work a cure. At any rate, they are most disgusting and repulsive to the occultist who beholds them in the human aura, and he often wonders why they do not sicken the person manifesting them – they often do just this thing, to tell the truth.

The Yellow Group. In this group of astral colors seen in the human aura we find as many varieties as we do in the red group. Yellow, denoting intellect, has many degrees of shade and tint, and many degrees of clearness.

An interesting shade in this group is that of orange, which represents different forms of "pride of intellect," intellectual ambition, love of mastery by will, etc. The greater degree of red in the astral orange color, the greater the connection with the physical or animal nature. Pride and love of power over others have much red in its astral color, while love of intellectual mastery has much less red in its composition.

Pure intellectual attainment, and the love of the same, is manifested by a beautiful clear golden yellow. Great teachers often have this so strongly in evidence that at times their students have glimpses of a golden "halo" around the head of the teacher. Teachers of great spirituality have this "nimbus" of golden yellow, with a border of beautiful blue tint, strongly in evidence.

The paintings of the great spiritual teachers of the race usually have this radiance pictured as a "halo," showing recognition of the phenomenon on the part of the great artists. Hoffman's celebrated painting of the Christ in the Garden of Gethsemane shows this nimbus so accurately depicted that the occultist is convinced that this artist must have actually witnessed a similar scene in the astral light, so true to the astral facts are its details. The images of the Buddha also show this radiance.

The rich golden shades of intellectual yellow are comparatively rare, a sickly lemon color being the only indication of intellectual power and found in the aura of the great run of persons. To the sight of the occultist, employing his power of astral vision, a crowd of persons will manifest here and there, at widely separated points, the bright golden yellow of the true intellect, appearing like scattered lighted candles among a multitude of faintly burning matches.

The Green Group. This is a peculiar group, consisting as of course it does of various combinations of blues and yellows, tinted and shaded by white or black. Even skilled occultists find it very difficult to account for the fact of certain green shades arising from the spiritual blue and the intellectual yellow. This is one of the most obscure points in the whole subject of the astral colors, and none but the most advanced occultists are able to explain the "why" in some instances. To those who are fond of analysis of this kind, I will drop the following hint, which may help them out in the matter...the key is found in the fact that green lies in the center of the astral spectrum and is a balance between the two extremes, and is also influenced by these two extremes in a startling manner.

A certain restful green denotes love of nature, out of door life, travel in the country, etc., and also, slightly differing in tint, the love of home scenes, etc. Again, a clear beautiful lighter tint of green indicates what may be called sympathy, altruistic emotion, charity, etc. Again, illustrating variety in this group of astral colors, another shade of green shows intellectual tolerance of the views of others. Growing duller, this indicates tact, diplomacy, ability to handle human nature, and descending another degree or so blends into insincerity, shiftiness, untruth, etc. There is an ugly slate-colored green indicating low, tricky deceit — this is a very common shade in the colors of the average aura, I am sorry to say. Finally, a particularly ugly, muddy, murky green indicates jealousy and kindred feelings, envious malice, etc.

The Blue Group. This interesting group of astral colors represents the varying forms and degrees of religious emotion, "spirituality," etc. The highest form of spiritual, religious feeling and thought is represented by a beautiful, rich, clear violet tint, while the lower and more gross phases of religious emotion and thought are represented by the darker and duller hues, tints and shades until a deep, dark indigo is reached, so dark that it can scarcely be distinguished from a bluish black. This latter color, as might be expected, indicates a low superstitious form of religion, scarcely worthy of the latter name. Religion, we must remember, has its low places as well as its heights; their gardens grow the rarest flowers and at the same time the vilest weeds.

High spiritual feelings, true spiritual unfoldment, are indicated by a wonderfully clear light blue, of an unusual tint, something akin to the clear light blue of the sky on a cool autumn afternoon, just before sunset. Even when we witness an approach to this color in nature, we are inspired by an uplifting feeling as if we were in the presence of higher things, so true is the intuition regarding these things.

Morality, of a high degree, is indicated by a series of beautiful shades of blue, always of a clear, inspiring tint. Religious feeling ruled by fear is indicated by a shade of bluish gray. Purple denotes a love of form and ceremony, particularly those connected with religious offices or regal grandeur of a solemn kind. Purple, naturally, was chosen as the royal color in the olden days.

The Brown Group. The brown group of astral colors represents desire for gain and accumulation, ranging from the clear brown of industrious accumulation, to the murky dull browns of miserliness, greed and avarice. There is a great range in this group of brown shades, as may be imagined.

The Gray Group. The group of grays represents a negative group of thought and emotions. Gray represents fear, depression, lack of courage, negativity, etc. This is an undesirable and unpleasant group.

Black. Black, in the astral colors, stands for hatred, malice, revenge and "devilishness" generally. It shades the brighter colors into their lower aspects, and robs them of their beauty. It stands for hate — also for gloom, depression, pessimism, etc.

White. White is the astral color of Pure Spirit, as we have seen, and its presence raises the degree of the other colors and renders them clearer. In fact, the perception of the highest degree of Being known to the most advanced occultist is manifested to the highest adepts and masters in the form of "The Great White Light," which transcends any light ever witnessed by the sight of man on either physical or astral plane, for it belongs to a plane higher than either and is absolute, rather than a relative, white. The presence of white among the astral colors of the human aura betokens a high degree of spiritual attainment and unfoldment, and when seen permeating the entire aura it is one of the signs of the master, the token of adeptship.

THE AURIC KALEIDOSCOPE

As we have seen, the human aura is never in a state of absolute rest or quiet. Motion and change are ever manifested by it. It has its periods of comparative calm, of course, but even in this state there is a pulsing, wave-like motion apparent. The clouds of changing color fly over its surface and in its depth like the fast driven fleecy clouds over the summer sky, illumined by the rays of the setting sun.

Again, fierce storms of mental activity, of emotional stress, disturb its comparative calm, and the wildest scenes are witnessed in the aura by the observer. So intense are the vibrations of some of these mental storms that their effect is plainly felt by the average person, though he is not able to distinguish the colors of the great whirls and swirls of auric substance accompanying them.

A person sunk in reverie, dream states or sleep presents an interesting auric kaleidoscope which possesses great beauty if the person be normal and of average morality. In such a case there is a cloudy clearness (if the term may be used) tinged with tints and shades of varying colors, blending in strange and interesting combinations, appearing gradually from previous combinations and sinking gradually into new ones.

To the observer of the aura the term opalescent distinctly presents itself, for there is a striking resemblance to the opaline peculiar play of colors of delicate tints and shades in a body of pearly or milky hue. Color shades into color, tint into tint, hue into hue, as in the color scale of the spectrum of which the rainbow is the most familiar example. But the rainbow or spectrum lacks the peculiar semi-transparency of the auric colors, and also the constantly changing and dissolving body of colors of the aura.

At this point I wish to call your attention to a phase of the aura which I purposely passed over in the preceding chapters. I allude to the phase of the aura which presents the "pearly" appearance of the opalescent body, which we have just noted. This appearance is manifested neither by any of the mental or emotional states, nor is it the prana-aura or vital force which I have described in a previous chapter. It is the manifestation of what is known to occultists as "etheric substance" and is a very interesting feature of the auric phenomena.

This etheric substance, which manifests this peculiar radiance in the body of the aura, composes that which is called by some occultists "the astral body," but this latter term is also employed in another sense, and I prefer to use the term "etheric double" to indicate what some others know as "the astral body." Etheric substance is much finer form of substance than that which composes the physical body. It is really matter in a very high degree of vibration – much higher than even the ultragaseous matter of physical substance. It may be sensed, ordinarily, only on the astral plane, which is its own particular plane of activity.

The etheric double, composed of this etheric substance, is the exact counterpart of its physical counterpart, the ordinary physical body of the individual, although it is capable of great expansion or shrinking in space. Like the physical body, it radiates an aura, and this combining with the other forms of the auric body gives to it its peculiar pearly appearance, which is the background of its opalescence previously noted.

The etheric double explains the phenomenon of spectral appearances or ghosts, for it persists for a time after the death of the physical body and under some conditions becomes visible to the ordinary sight. It sometimes is projected from the physical body and at such times appears as an apparition of the living, of which there are many cases recorded by the societies investigating psychical subjects.

The etheric double, or astral body, is referred to here, however, merely to explain the peculiar pearly tint of the background, or body, of the aura in and through which the mental and emotional auric colors play and move. It may interest you, however, to know that this phase of aura is always present around and about a "ghost" or dematerialized disembodied soul, or "spirit," as common usage terms it.

The aura of the wide-awake person is far more active and more deeply colored than is that of the person in reverie, dream or sleep. And again, the aura of the person manifesting a high degree of mental activity or strong feeling or passion is still brighter and deeper than the ordinary person performing his daily routine work. In the state of anger, or love-passion, for instance, the aura is violently disturbed, deep shades of color whirling and swirling in the depths and surface of the auric body. Lightning-like flashes shoot forth, and great bodies of lurid smoky clouds fly on the surface. Looking into the aura of a man wild with rage and passion is like peering into Inferno. The astral plane in the region of a lynching mob or other body of persons filled with rage becomes a frightful scene of auric radiation.

A person filled with the emotion of pure love fills his aura with the most beautiful tints and shades of high rosy color, and to behold the same is a pleasure fully appreciated by the occultist. A church filled with persons of high devotional ideals is also a beautiful place, by reason of the mingling of auric violet-blue vibrations of those therein assembled.

The atmosphere of a jail or prison can be most depressing and presents an unpleasant appearance to one possessing the astral vision. Likewise, the astral atmosphere of a house of prostitution, or other dens of iniquity, becomes physically nauseating to the occultist of high ideals and taste. Such scenes on the astral plane are avoided by all true occultists, except when the call of duty leads them to visit them to give aid and help.

There are two distinct features connected with the auric coloring of every person. The first is the coloring resulting from the more habitual thoughts and feelings of the person from his character, in fact; while the second is the coloring resulting from the particular feelings or thoughts manifested by him at that particular moment or time.

The color of the feeling of the moment soon disappears and fades away, while the more habitual feeling, bound up with his character, causes its corresponding color to abide more permanently and thus to give a decided hue to his general auric color appearance.

The trained occultist is, therefore, able to ascertain not only the passing thoughts and feelings of a person, but also to determine infallibly his general character, tendencies, past character and actions, and general nature simply from a careful examination and study of the auric colors of the person in question.

As all occultists well know, every place, dwelling, business place, church, courtroom--every village, city, country, and nation – has its own collective aura, known as "astral atmosphere," which is simply but a combined reflection of the individual auras of the human units of which its body of inhabitants is made up. These atmospheric vibrations are plainly felt by many persons, and we are instinctively attracted or repelled by reason thereof. But to the developed occultists, these places manifest the auric colors in the combinations arising from the nature of the mentalities of the persons dwelling in them.

PARA-X POWERS

Each place has its collective aura, just as each person has his individual aura. The astral plane presents a wonderful scene of color by reason of this and similar causes. The harmony of the color scheme in some cases is marvellously beautiful, while the horrible aspect of scenes resemble a nightmare vision of the worst kind.

It is easy to understand why some of the ancients who stumbled into glimpses of the astral plane, while in dream-state or trance, reported the vision of terrible hells of unquenchable fire, fiery lakes of smoking brimstone, etc., for such ideas would naturally come to the mind of the uninformed person who had peered into the astral plane in such cases. And in the same way, the visions of heaven reported by the saints and others of high spirituality are explainable on the theory that these persons had sensed some of the beautiful scenes of the higher astral planes, filled with the combined auric tints and hues of souls of high development. The principle of auric colors holds on all the many planes of being and existence – high as well as low.

I merely hint at a great occult truth in making the above statements. The thoughtful will be able to read between my lines. I have given you a little key which will unlock the door of many mysteries, if you will but use it intelligently.

THOUGHT FORMS

That interesting phase of occult phenomena known as thought forms is so closely related to the general subject of the human aura that a mention of one must naturally lead to the thought of the other. Thought forms are built up of the very material composing the aura, and manifest the entire general characteristics thereof, even to the auric colors. An understanding of the facts of the human aura is necessary for a correct understanding of the nature of the thought forms composed of the same substance.

A thought form is a peculiar manifestation of mental activity on the astral plane. It is more than a powerful disturbance in the body of the human aura, although this is the place of its embodiment or birth in the objective world. It is formed in the following manner. A person manifests a strong desire, feeling or idea which is naturally filled with the dynamic force of his will. This sets up a series of strong vibrations in the body of the aura which gradually resolve themselves into a strong whirling center of thought force involved in a mass of strongly cohesive auric substance and strongly charged with the power of the prana of the person.

151

In some cases these thought forms survive in the auric body for some little time and then gradually fade away. In other cases they survive and maintain an almost independent existence for some time and exert a strong influence upon other persons coming in the presence of the person. Again, these thought forms may be so strongly charged with prana and so imbued with the mental force of the person that they will actually be thrown off and away from the aura itself and travel in space until they exhaust their initial energy – in the meantime exerting an influence upon the psychic aura of other persons.

A thought form is more than merely a strongly manifested thought, it really is such a thought but surrounded by a body of ethereal substance, charged with prana and even carrying with it the vibration of the life energy of its creator. It is a child of the mind of its creator and acquires a portion of his life-essence, so to speak, which abides with it for a longer or shorter time after its birth. In extreme instances it becomes practically a semi-living elemental force of necessarily comparatively short life.

To those who find it difficult to understand how a thought form can persist after separation from the presence of the thinker, I would say that the phenomenon is similar to that of light traveling in space, long after the star which originated it has been destroyed. Or, again, it is like the vibrations of heat remaining in a room after the lamp or stove causing it has been removed, or the fire in the grate having died out, or like the sound waves of the drum-beat persisting after the beat itself has ceased. It is all a matter of the persistence of vibrations.

Thought forms differ greatly from one to the other in the matter of shape and general appearance. The most common and simple form is that of an undulating wave or series of tiny waves resembling the circles caused by the dropping of a pebble into a still pond. Another form is that of a tiny rotating bit of cloud-like substance, sometimes whirling towards a central point, like a whirlpool, and sometimes swirling away from the central point like the familiar "pinwheel" fireworks toy.

Another form is akin the ring of smoke projected from the coughing locomotive, or the rounded lips of the cigar smoker, the movement in this kind being a form of spiral rotation. Other thought forms have the appearance of swiftly rotating balls of cloudy substance, often glowing with faint phosphorescence.

Sometimes the thought form will appear as a great slender jet, like steam ejected from the spout of a tea-kettle, which is sometimes broken up into a series of short, puffed out jets, each following the jet preceding it and traveling in a straight line. Sometimes the thought form shoots forth like a streak of dim light, almost resembling a beam of light flashed from a mirror. Occasionally, it will twist its way along like a long, slender corkscrew, or auger, boring into space.

In cases of thought forms sent forth by explosive emotion, the thought form will actually take the form of a bomb, which literally explodes when it reaches the presence of the person toward whom it is aimed. Every person has experienced this feeling of a thought bomb having been exploded in his near vicinity, having been directed by a vigorous personality. This form is frequently found in the thought forms sent out by a strong, earnest, vigorous orator.

There are strong thought forms which seem to strive to push back the other person, so correctly do they represent the idea and feeling back of their manifestation. Others seem to strive to wind around the other person and to try to literally drag him toward the first person, this form often accompanying strong appeal, persuasion, coaxing, etc., when accompanied by strong desire. A particularly vigorous form of this kind of thought form takes on the appearance of a nebulous octopus with long, winding, clinging tentacles, striving to wrap around the other person and to draw him toward the center.

The force of the feeling behind the manifestation of the thought form will often travel a long distance from the sender--in fact, in cases of great power of concentration, space seems to be no barrier to its passage. In striking instances of thought transference, etc., it will be found that thought forms play an important part.

The variety of shapes of thought forms is almost endless. Each combination of thought and feeling creates its own form, and each individual seems to have his own peculiarities in this respect. The forms I have above described, however, will serve as typical cases to illustrate the more common classes of appearances. The list, however, might be indefinitely expanded from the experience of any experienced occultist and is not intended to be full by any means. All varieties of geometrical forms are found among the thought forms, some of them being of remarkable beauty.

In considering the subject of projected thought forms, moreover, it must be remembered that they partake of and manifest the same colors as does the aura itself, for they are composed of the same material and are charged with the same energy. But note this difference, that whereas the aura is energized from the constant battery of the organism of the individual, the thought form, on the contrary, has at its service only the energy with which it was charged when it was thrown off, being a storage battery, as it were, which in time expends all of its power and then is powerless.

Every thought form bears the same color that it would possess if it had been retained in the body of the aura itself. But as a rule, the colors are plainer and less blended with others, this because each thought form is the representation of a single definite feeling or thought, or group of same, instead of being a body of widely differing mental vibrations. Thus, the thought form of anger will show its black and red with its characteristic flashes. The thought form of passion will show forth its appropriate auric colors and general characteristics. The thought form of high ideal love will show its beautiful form and harmonious tinting, like a wonderful celestial flower from the garden of some far-off paradise.

Many thought forms never leave the outer limits of the aura, while others are projected to great distances. Some sputter out as they travel and are disintegrated, while others continue to glow like a piece of heated iron for many hours. Others persist for a long time, with a faint phosphorescent glow. A careful study of what has been said regarding the characteristics of the various feelings and emotions as manifested in the auric body will give the student a very fair general idea of what may be the appearance of any particular variety of thought form, for a general principle runs through the entire series of auric phenomena. An understanding of the fundamental principles will lead to an understanding of any of the particular varieties of the manifestation thereof.

Finally, remember this: a thought form is practically a bit of the detached aura of a person, charged with a degree of his prana and energized with a degree of his life energy. So, in a limited sense, it really is a projected portion of his personality.

PSYCHIC INFLUENCE OF COLORS

In all of nature's wonderful processes we find many evidences of that great principle of action and reaction, which, like the forward and backward swing of the pendulum, changes cause into effect, and effect into cause, in a never ending series. We find this principle in effect in the psychic relation of mental states and colors. That is to say that just as we find that certain mental and emotional states manifest in vibrations causing particular auric astral colors, so do we find that the presence of certain colors on the physical plane will have a decided psychic effect upon the mental and emotional states of individuals subject to their influence. And as might be expected by the thoughtful student, the particular astral colors manifested in the aura by the presence of some particular mental or emotional state exactly correspond with the particular physical colors which influence that particular mental or emotional state.

Illustrating the statements in the preceding paragraph, I would say that the continued presence of red will be apt to set up emotional vibrations of anger, passion, physical love, etc., or in a different tint, the higher physical emotions. Blue of the right tint will tend to cause feelings of spirituality, religious emotion, etc. Green is conducive to feelings of relaxation, repose, quiet, etc. Black produces the feeling of gloom and grief. And so on, each color tends to produce emotional vibrations similar to those which manifest that particular color in the astral aura of the person. It is a case of "give and take" along the entire scale of color and emotions, according to the great natural laws.

While the explanation of these facts is not known to the average person, nevertheless nearly everyone recognizes the subtle effect of color and avoids certain colors, while seeking certain others. There is not a single living human being but who has experienced the sense of rest, calm, repose and calm inflow of strength when in a room decorated in quiet shades of green.

Nature herself has given this particular shade to the grass and leaves of trees and plants, so that the soothing effect of the country scene is produced. The aura of a person experiencing these feelings and yielding to them will manifest precisely the tint or shade of green which is shown on the grass and leaves around him, so true is this natural law of action and reaction.

The effect of scarlet upon animals, the bull for instance, is well known, to use the familiar term, it causes one to "see red." The sight of the color of blood is apt to arouse feelings of rage, or disgust, by reason of the same law. The sight of the beautiful clear blue sky tends to arouse feelings of reverence, awe or spirituality. One can never think of this shade of blue arousing rage; or red arousing feelings of spirituality.

It is a well-known fact that in insane asylums, the use of red in decorations must be avoided, while the proper shades of blue or green are favored. On the other hand, the use of a proper red in certain cases will tend to arouse vitality and physical strength in a patient. It is not by mere chance that the life-giving blood is a bright, rich red color when it leaves the heart.

When one "feels blue" he does not have the impression of a bright or soft blue, but he really is almost conscious of the presence of a dull bluish gray. And the presence of such a color in one's surroundings tends to cause a feeling of depression. Everyone knows the "gray day" in the fall or spring.

Again, who does not know the feeling of mental exaltation coming from the sight of a day filled with golden sunshine or from a golden sunset? We find proofs of this law of nature on all sides, every day of our lives. It is an interesting subject which will repay the student for the expenditure of a little time and thought upon it.

Speaking of the general class characteristics of the three primary groups of colors, all occultists, as well as many physiologists and psychologists, are agreed on the following fundamental propositions: (1) red is exciting to the mind and emotions; (2) yellow is inspiring and elevating and intellectually stimulating; and (3) blue is cool, soothing and calming. It is also universally conceded that the right shades of green (combining the qualities of blue and yellow in appropriate proportions) is the ideal color of rest and recuperation, followed by a stimulation and new ambition. The reason for this may be seen when you consider the respective qualities of blue and yellow, which compose this color.

It is interesting to note that the science of medicine is now seriously considering the use of colors in the treatment of disease, and the best medical authorities investigating the subject are verifying the teachings of the old occultists regarding the influence of colors on mental states and physical conditions.

Dr. Edwin Babbitt, a pioneer in this line in the Western world, gave the general principles in a nutshell when he laid down the following rule: "There is a trianal series of graduations in the peculiar potencies of colors, the center and climax of electrical action, which cools the nerves, being in violet; the climax of electrical action, which is soothing to the vascular system, being in blue; the climax of luminosity being in yellow; and the climax of thermism, or heat, being in red. This is not an imaginary division of qualities, but a real one, the flame-like red color having a principle of warmth in itself; the blue and violet, a principle of cold and electricity. Thus we have many styles of chromatic action, including progression of hues, of lights and shades, of fineness and coarseness, of electrical power, luminous power, thermal power, etc."

Read the above statement of Dr. Babbitt and then compare it with the occult teaching regarding the astral colors, and you will perceive the real basis of the science which the good doctor sought to establish and in which cause he did such excellent pioneer work. The result of his work is now being elaborated by modern physicians in the great schools of medicine, particularly in Europe...England and America being somewhat behind the times in this work.

The advanced occultist also finds much satisfaction in the interest on the part of physicians and jurists in the matter of the influence of color upon the mental, moral and physical welfare of

PARA-X POWERS

the public. The effect of color upon morality is being noticed by workers for human welfare occupying important offices.

The American journals report the case of a judge in a large Western city in that country who insisted upon his courtroom being decorated in light, cheerful tints, instead of in the old, gloomy, depressing shades formerly employed. This judge wisely remarked that brightness led to right thinking, and darkness to crooked thinking; also that his court, being an uplift court, must have walls to correspond, and that it was enough to turn any man into a criminal to be compelled to sit in a dark, dismal courtroom day after day.

This good judge, who must have had some acquaintance with the occult teachings, is quoted as concluding as follows: "White, cream, light yellow and orange are the colors which are the sanest. I might add light green, for that is the predominant color in nature; black, brown and deep red are incentives to crime, a man in anger sees red." Surely a remarkable utterance from the bench.

The effect of color schemes upon the moral and mental welfare of persons is being recognized in the direction of providing brighter color schemes in schools, hospitals, reformatories, prisons, etc. The reports naturally show the correctness of the underlying theory. The color of a tiny flower has its effect upon even the most hardened prisoner, while the minds of children in school are quickened by a touch of brightness here and there in the room. It needs no argument to prove the beneficial effect of the right kind of colors in the sickroom or hospital ward.

The prevailing theories and practice regarding the employment of color in therapeutics and human welfare work are in the main correct. But I urge the study of the occult significance of color, as mentioned in this book in connection with the human aura and its astral colors, as a sound basis for an intelligent, thorough understanding of the real psychic principles underlying the physical application of the methods referred to. Go to the center of the subject and then work outward--that is the true rule of the occultist which might well be followed by the non-occult general public.

AURIC MAGNETISM

The phenomenon of human magnetism is too well recognized by the general public to require argument at this time. Let the expert's dispute about it as much as they please, down in the heart of nearly all of the plain people of the race is the conviction that there is such a thing. The occultists, of course, are quite familiar with the wonderful manifestations of this great natural force, and

157

with its effect upon the minds and bodies of members of the race, and can afford to smile at the attempts of some of the narrow minds in the colleges to pooh-pooh the matter.

But the average person is not familiar with the relation of this human magnetism to the human aura. I think that the student should familiarize himself with this fundamental relation in order to reason correctly on the subject of human magnetism.

Here is the fundamental fact in a nutshell: the human aura is the great storehouse, or reservoir, of human magnetism, and is the source of all human magnetism that is projected by the individual toward other individuals. Just how human magnetism is generated is, of course, a far deeper matter, but it is enough for our purpose at this time to explain the fact of its storage and transmission.

In cases of magnetic healing, etc., the matter is comparatively simple. In such instances the healer by an effort of the will (sometimes unconsciously applied) projects a supply of his pranic aura vibrations into the body of his patient by way of the nervous system of the patient and also by means of what may be called the induction of the aura itself.

The mere presence of a person strongly charged with prana is often enough to cause an overflow into the aura of other persons, with a resulting feeling of new strength and energy. By the use of the hands of the healer, a heightened effect is produced by reason of certain properties inherent in the nervous system of both healer and patient.

There is even a flow of etheric substance from the aura of the healer to that of the patient in cases where the vitality of the latter is very low. Many a healer has actually and literally pumped his life force and etheric substance into the body of his patient when the latter was sinking into the weakness which precedes death and has by so doing been able to bring him back to life and strength. This is practically akin to the transfusion of blood, except that it is on the psychic plane instead of the physical.

But the work of the magnetic healer does not stop here if he be well informed regarding his science. The educated healer, realizing the potent effect of mental states upon physical conditions of mental vibrations upon the physical nerve centers and organs of the body — endeavors to arouse the proper mental vibrations in the mind of his patient.

Ordinarily he does this merely by holding in his mind the corresponding desired mental state and thus arousing similar vibrations in the mind of the patient. This, of itself, is a powerful weapon of healing and constitutes the essence of mental healing as usually practiced. But there is a possible improvement even upon this, as we shall see in a moment.

PARA-X POWERS

/ The advanced occultist, realizing the law of action and reaction in the matter of the auric colors, turns the same to account in healing work, as follows. He not only holds in his mind the strong feeling and thought which he wishes to transmit to the patient, but (fix this in your mind) he also pictures in his imagination the particular kind of color which corresponds with the feeling or thought in question.

A moment's thought will show you that by this course he practically multiplies the effect. Not only do his own thought vibrations (1) set up corresponding vibrations in the mind of the patient by the laws of thought transference, but (2) his thought of the certain colors will set up corresponding vibrations not only (a) in his own aura, and thence (b) to that of the patient, but will also (3) act directly upon the aura of the patient and reproduce the colors there, which (4) in turn will arouse corresponding vibrations in the mind of the patient by the law of reaction.

The above may sound a little complicated at first reading, but a little analysis will show you that it is really quite a simple process, acting strictly along the lines of action and reaction, which law has been explained to you in preceding chapters of this book. The vibrations rebound from mind to aura, and from aura to mind, in the patient, something like a billiard ball flying from one side of the table to another, or a tennis ball flying between the two racquets over the net.

The principle herein mentioned may be employed as well in what is called "absent treatment," as in treatments where the patient is present. By the laws of thought transference, not only the thought but also the mental image of the appropriate astral color is transmitted over space and then, impinging on the mind of the patient, is transmitted into helpful and health giving vibrations in his mind. The healer of any school of mental or spiritual healing will find this plan very helpful to him in giving absent as well as present treatments. I recommend it from years of personal experience, as well as that of other advanced occultists.

Of course, the fact that the ordinary healer is not able to distinguish the finer shades of astral color, by reason of his not having actually perceived them manifested in the aura, renders his employment of this method less efficacious than that of the developed and trained occultist. But nevertheless, he will find that from the knowledge of the auric or astral colors given in this little book he will be able to obtain quite satisfactory and marked results in his practice. The following table, committed to memory, will be of help to him in the matter of employing the mental image of the auric colors in his healing work.

PARA-X POWERS

TABLE OF HEALING COLORS

Nervous System:
Cooling and soothing: shades of violet, lavender, etc.
Resting and invigorating effect: grass greens.
Inspiring and illuminating: medium yellows and orange.
Stimulating and exciting: reds (bright).

Blood and Organs:
Cooling and soothing: clear, dark blues.
Resting and invigorating: grass greens.
Inspiring and illuminating: orange yellows.
Stimulating and exciting: bright reds.

The following additional suggestions will be found helpful to the healer. In cases of impaired physical vitality, also chilliness, lack of bodily warmth, etc., bright, warm reds are indicated. In cases of feverishness, overheated blood, excessive blood pressure, inflammation, etc., blue is indicated. Red has a tendency to produce renewed and more active heart action, while violets and lavenders tend to slow down the too rapid beating of the heart.

A nervous, unstrung patient may be treated by bathing her mentally in a flood of violet or lavender auric color, while a tired, used up, fatigued person may be invigorated by flooding him with bright reds, followed by bright, rich yellows, finishing the treatment with a steady flow of warm orange color.

To those who are sufficiently advanced in occult philosophy, I would say that they should remember the significance of the Great White Light and accordingly conclude their treatment by an effort to indicate an approach to that clear, pure white color in the aura – mentally, of course. This will leave the patient in an inspired, exalted, illuminated state of mind and soul, which will be of great benefit to him, and will also have the effect of reinvigorating the healer by cosmic energy or para-prana.

Everything that has been said in this chapter regarding the use of color in magnetic treatments is equally applicable to cases of self-healing or self-treatment. Let the patient follow the directions above given for the healer and then turn the healing current, or thought, inward – and the result will be the same as if he were treating another. The individual will soon find that certain colors fit his requirements better than others, in which case let him follow such experience in preference to general rules, for the intuition generally is the safest guide in such cases. However, it will be found that the individual experience will usually agree with the tables given above, with slight personal variations.

PARA-X POWERS

DEVELOPING THE AURA

When it is remembered that the aura of the individual affects and influences other persons with whom he comes in contact, and is, in fact, an important part of his personality, it will be seen that it is important that the individual take pains to develop his aura in the direction of desirable qualities and to neutralize and weed out undesirable ones. This becomes doubly true when it is also remembered that, according to the law of action and reaction, the auric vibrations react upon the mind of the individual, thus intensifying and adding fuel to the original mental states which called them forth. From any point of view, it is seen to be an important part of self development and character building to develop the aura according to scientific occult principles.

In this work of aura development there are found to be two correlated phases, namely: (1) the direct work of flooding the aura with the best vibrations, by means of holding in the mind clear, distinct and repeated mental pictures of desirable ideas and feelings; and (2) the added effect of mental images of the colors corresponding to the ideas and feelings which are deemed desirable and worthy of development.

The first of the above-mentioned phases is probably far more familiar to the average student than is the second. This from the fact that the average student is apt to be more or less familiar with the teachings of the numerous schools or cults which agree in the axiom that "holding the thought" tends to develop the mind of the individual along the particular lines of such thought.

This is a correct psychological principle, for that matter, even when those practicing it do not fully understand the underlying facts. Mental faculties, like physical muscles, tend to develop by exercise and use, and any faculty may be developed and cultivated in this way.

Another teaching of these same schools is that the character of the thoughts so "held" by the individual affects other persons with whom he comes in contact, and in a way attracts to him objective things, persons and circumstances in harmony with such thoughts. This also is in accordance with the best occult teaching, from which, of course, it was originally derived. I heartily endorse the facts of these teachings and pronounce them fundamentally correct. And in this connection I may say that every healer may apply his own methods plus this teaching regarding the aura, and thus obtain greatly increased results.

By the faithful, persevering holding in mind of certain ideas and feelings, the individual may flood his aura with the vibrations and colors of such ideas and feelings, and thus charge it with auric energy and power. By so doing, he gains the benefit of the reaction upon his own mind, and also secures the advantage of the affect thereof upon other persons with whom he comes in contact. In this way he not only builds up his individual character along desirable lines, but at the same time develops a strong, positive, attractive "personality" which affects others with whom he comes in contact.

I do not consider it necessary to go into details here regarding this phase of "holding the thought," for as I have said, the average student is already familiar with the rules regarding the same. In a nutshell, however, I will say that each individual is largely the result of the thoughts he has manifested and the feelings which he has harbored. Therefore, the rule is to manifest and exercise the faculties you would develop, and inhibit or refrain from manifesting the ones you would restrain or control.

Again, to restrain an undesirable faculty, develop and exercise its opposite, kill out the negatives by developing the positives. The mind produces thought; and yet it tends to grow from the particular portion of its own product which you may choose to feed to it, for it not only creates thought, but also feeds upon it. So, finally, let it produce the best kind of thought for you, and then throw that back into the hopper, for it will use it to grind out more of the same kind and grow strong in so doing. That is the whole thing in a nutshell.

The second phase of aura development (as above classified), however, is not likely to be familiar to the average student for the reason that it is not known outside of advanced occult circles, and very little has been allowed to be taught regarding it. But the very reticence regarding it is a proof of its importance, and I strongly advise my students to give to it the attention and practice that its importance merits. The practice thereof, however, is extremely simple, and the principle of the practice, moreover, is based solely upon the facts of the relation of color and mental states, as shown in the astral auric colors.

In order to intelligently practice the development of the aura by means of flooding or charging it with the vibrations of psychic colors, it is first necessary that the student be thoroughly familiar with the scale of colors related to each set of mental states or emotional feelings.

The student should turn back the pages of this chapter and then carefully reread and re-study every word which has been said about the relation of mental states and auric colors. He should know the mental correspondence of the shades of red, yellow and blue so thoroughly that the thought of one will bring the idea of the other. He should be able to think of the corresponding group of colors the moment he thinks of any particular mental state. He should be thoroughly familiar with the physical, mental and spiritual effect of any of the colors, and should, moreover, test himself psychically for the individual effects of certain colors upon himself.

He should enter into this study with interest and earnestness, and then by keeping his eyes and ears open, he will perceive interesting facts concerning the subject on every side in his daily work and life. He will perceive many proofs of the principle and will soon amass a stock of experiences illustrating each color and its corresponding mental state. He will be richly repaid for the work of such study, which, in fact, will soon grow to be more like pleasure than like work.

Having mastered this phase of the subject, the student should give himself a thorough, honest, self-examination and mental analysis. He should write down a chart of his strong points and his weak ones. He should check off the traits which should be developed and those which should be restrained. He should determine whether he needs development along physical, mental and spiritual lines, and in what degree. Having made this chart of himself, he should then apply the principles of charging the aura with the color vibrations indicated by his self diagnosis and prescription.

The last stage is quite simple, once one has acquired the general idea behind it. It consists simply in forming as clear a mental image as possible of the color or colors desired and then projecting the vibrations into the aura by the simple effort of the will. Willing, in the occult sense, may be said to consist of a command, leaving the rest to the mechanism of the will and mind. Take away the obstacle of doubt and fear – then the Royal Command performs the work of setting the will into operation. This, by the way, is an important occult secret of wide application – try to master its all-important significance.

The mental imaging of colors may be materially aided by concentration upon physical material of the right color. By concentrating the attention and vision upon a red flower, for instance, or upon a bit of green leaf in another instance, one may be able to form a clear, positive mental image of that particular color. This accompanied by the willing and demand that the vibrations of this color shall charge the aura will be found to accomplish the result. Have something around you showing the desirable colors, and your attention will almost instinctively take up the impression thereof, even though you may be thinking or doing something else.

Live as much as possible in the idea and presence of the desirable color, and you will get the habit of setting up the mental image and vibration thereof. A little practice and experience will soon give you the idea and enable you to get the best results. Patience, perseverance and sustained earnest interest – that is the key of success.

THE PROTECTIVE AURA

Among the very oldest of the teachings of Para-X Power, we find instructions regarding the building up and maintenance of the protective aura of the individual, whereby he renders himself immune to undesirable physical, mental, psychic or spiritual influences. So important is this teaching that it is to be regretted that there has not been more said on the subject by some of the writers of recent years.

The trouble with many of these recent writers is that they seem to wish to close their eyes to the unpleasant facts of life, and to gaze only upon the pleasant ones. But this is a mistake, for ignorance has never been a virtue, and to shut one's eyes to unpleasant facts does not always result in destroying them. I consider any teaching unfinished and inadequate which does not include instruction along protective lines.

Physical auric protection consists in charging the aura with vital magnetism and color, which will tend to ward off not only the physical contagion of ill persons, but, what is often still more important, the contagion of their mind and feelings.

The student who has really studied this chapter will at once realize that this protection is afforded by filling the aura with the vibrations of health and physical strength, by means of the mental imaging of the life-preserving reds, and the exercise of the mind in the direction of thought of strength and power. These two things will tend to greatly increase the resistive aura of anyone, and enable him to throw off disease influences which affect others.

The aura of the successful physician and healer, in the presence of disease, will invariably show the presence of the bright, positive red in the aura, accompanied by the mental vibrations of strength, power and confidence, and the absence of fear. This in connection with the auric circle, which shall be described presently, will be of great value to healers, physicians, nurses, etc., as well as to those who are brought into intimate contact with sick persons.

Of practically the same degree of importance is the charging of the aura with the vibrations of mental protection, the vibrations of orange, yellow and similar colors. These are the colors of intellect, you will remember, and when the aura is charged and flooded with them it acts as a protection against the efforts of others to convince one against his will by arguments, plausible reasoning, fallacious illustrations, etc. It gives to one a sort of mental illumination, quickening the perceptive faculties and brightening up the reasoning and judging powers, and, finally, giving a sharp edge to the powers of repartee and answer.

If you will assume the right positive mental attitude, and will flood your aura with the vibrations of the mental orange-yellow, the mental efforts of other persons will rebound from your aura, or, to use another figure of speech, will slip from it like water from the back of the proverbial duck. It is well to carry the mental image of your head being surrounded by a golden aura or halo at such times, this will be found especially efficacious as a protective helmet when you are assaulted by the intellect or arguments of others.

And, again, there is a third form of protective aura, namely protection of one's emotional nature, and this is highly important when one remembers how frequently we are moved to action by our emotions, rather than by our intellect or reason. To guard one's emotions is to guard one's very inmost soul, so to speak. If we can protect our feeling and emotional side, we will be able to use our reasoning powers and intellect far more effectively, as all know by experience.

What color should we use in this form of auric protection? Can anyone be in doubt here if he has read the preceding chapters? What is the emotional protective color? Why, blue, of course. Blue controls this part of the mind or soul, and by raising ourselves into the vibrations of positive blue, we leave behind us the lower emotions and feelings and are transported into the higher realms of the soul where these low vibrations and influences cannot follow us. In the same way, the blue colored aura will act as an armor to protect us from the contagion of the low passions and feelings of others.

If you are subjected to evil influences or contagion of those harboring low emotions and desires, you will do well to acquire the art of flooding your aura with the positive blue tints. Make a study of bright, clear blues, and you will instinctively select the one best suited for your needs. Nature gives us this instinctive knowledge, if we will but seek for it, and then apply it when found.

The aura of great moral teachers, great priests and preachers, advanced occultists, in fact all men of lofty ideals working among those lower on the moral scale, are always found to be charged with a beautiful, clear blue which acts as a protection to them when they are unduly exposed to moral or emotional contagion.

Ignorance of the occult laws has caused the downfall of many a great moral teacher, who could have protected himself in this way, in times of strong attack of low vibrations, had he but known the truth. The individual who knows this law, and who applies it, is rendered absolutely immune from evil contagion on the emotional plane of being.

THE GREAT AURIC CIRCLE

But no instruction on this subject would be complete without a reference to the great auric circle of protection, which is a shelter to the soul, mind and body against outside psychic influences directed consciously or unconsciously against the individual. In these days of widespread though imperfect knowledge of psychic phenomena and Para-X Power, it is especially important that one should be informed as to this great shield of protection. Omitting all reference to the philosophy underlying it, it may be said that this auric circle is formed by making the mental image, accompanied by the demand of will, of the aura being surrounded by a great band of pure clear white light. A little perseverance will enable you to create this on the astral plane, and though (unless you have the astral vision) you cannot see it actually, yet you will actually feel its protective presence so that you will know that it is there guarding you.

This white auric circle will be an effective and infallible armor against all forms of psychic attack or influence, no matter from whom it may emanate, or whether directed consciously or unconsciously. It is a perfect and absolute protection, and the knowledge of its protective power should be sufficient to drive fear from the heart of all who have dreaded psychic influence, "malicious animal magnetism" (so-called), or anything else of the kind, by whatever name known. It is also a protection against psychic vampirism, or draining of magnetic strength.

The auric circle is, of course, really egg-shaped, or oval, for it fringes the aura as the shell cases the egg. See yourself, mentally, as surrounded by this great white auric circle of protection, and let the idea sink into your consciousness. Realize its power over the influences from outside, and rejoice in the immunity it gives you.

The auric circle, however, will admit any outside impressions that you really desire to come to you, while shutting out the others. That is, with this exception, that if your inner soul recognizes that some of these desired influences and impressions are apt to harm you (though your reason and feeling know it not) then will such impressions be denied admittance.

PARA-X POWERS

For the white light is the radiation of spirit, which is higher than ordinary mind, emotion or body and is master of all. And its power, even though we can but imperfectly represent it even mentally, is such that before its energy, and in its presence, in the aura, all lower vibrations are neutralized and disintegrated.

13
PARA-X POWER IN EVERYDAY LIFE

SCIENTISTS speak of the Law of Gravitation, but ignore that equally wonderful manifestation, The Law of Attraction. We are familiar with that wonderful manifestation of Law which draws and holds together the atoms of which matter is composed - we recognize the power of the law that attracts bodies to the earth, that holds the circling worlds in their places, but we close our eyes to **the mighty law that draws to us the things we desire or fear, that makes or mars our lives.**

With Para-X Power, we see that Thought is a force – a manifestation of energy – having a magnet-like power of attraction. When we think we send out vibrations of a fine ethereal substance, which are as real as the vibrations manifesting light, heat, electricity, magnetism. That these vibrations are not evident to our five senses is no proof that they do not exist.

A powerful magnet will send out vibrations and exert a force sufficient to attract to itself a piece of steel weighing a hundred pounds, but we can neither see, taste, smell, hear nor feel the mighty force. These thought vibrations, likewise, cannot be seen, tasted, smelled, heard nor felt in the ordinary way; although it is true there are on record cases of persons peculiarly sensitive to psychic impressions who have perceived powerful thought-waves, and very many of us can testify that we have distinctly felt the thought vibrations of others, both whilst in the presence of the sender and at a distance. Telepathy and its kindred phenomena are not idle dreams.

We are all influenced much more than we are aware by the thoughts of others. I do not mean by their opinions but by their thoughts. A great writer on this subject very truly says: "thoughts are things." They are things, and most powerful things at that. Unless we understand this fact, we are at the mercy of a mighty force, of whose nature we know nothing, and whose very existence many of us deny. On the other hand, if we understand the nature and laws governing Para-X Power, we can master it and render it our instrument and assistant. Every thought created by us, weak or strong, good or bad, healthy or unhealthy, sends out its vibratory waves, which affect, to a greater or lesser extent all with whom we come in contact, or who may come within the radius of our thought vibrations. Thought waves are like the ripples on a pond caused by the casting in of a pebble, they move in constantly widening circles, radiating from a central point. Of course, if an impulse

PARA-X POWERS

projects the thought waves forcibly toward a certain object, its force will be felt more strongly at that point.

Besides affecting others, our thoughts affect us, not only temporarily, but also permanently. We are what we think ourselves into being. The biblical statement that "as a man thinketh in his heart, so is he," is literally correct. We are all creatures of our own mental creating.

You know how easy it is to think yourself into a funk, or the reverse, but you do not realized that repeated thought upon a certain line will manifest itself not only in character (which it certainly does), but also in the physical appearance of the thinker. This is a demonstrable fact, and you have but to look around you to realize it.

You have noticed how a man's occupation shows itself in his appearance and general character. What do you suppose occasions this phenomenon? Nothing more or less than that thought. If you've have changed your occupation, your general character and appearance kept pace with your changed habits of thought. Your new occupation brought out a new train of thought, and "Thoughts take form in Action." You may have never taken this view of the matter, but it is true nevertheless, and you may find ample proof of its correctness by merely looking around you.

A man who thinks Energy manifests Energy. The man who thinks Courage manifests courage. The man who thinks, "I can and I will," "gets there", while the "I can't" man "gets left." You know that to be true. Now, what causes the difference? Thought – just plain thought. Action follows as the natural result of vigorous thinking. You think in earnest, and action does the rest. Thought is the greatest thing in the world.

Your thought attracts to it the corresponding thought of others and increases your stock of that particular kind of thought. Think Fear thoughts, and you draw to yourself all the Fear thought in that neighborhood. The harder you think it, the greater supply of undesirable thought flocks to you. Think "I am Fearless," and all the courageous thought force within your radius will move towards you, and will aid you.

PARA-X POWER CAN HELP YOU IN MANY WAYS

Para-X Power, along with the power of thought, can be used in a number of ways in the direction of influencing others and gaining success. Para-X Power will aid you in the following manner:

PARA-X POWERS

1. By the use of your positive thought force in the direction of directly influencing men in person, through the law of Suggestion. By this I mean that you will be able to interest men in your schemes and plans, enlist their aid, secure their patron - age, and influence them generally. This faculty, natural to some men, can be acquired by any man or woman who has the will power and perseverance to develop it within them. Most students of the subject are desirous of acquiring knowledge of this branch of Mental Control before the other phases of the subject, and I, therefore, will take it up in my next lesson.

2. By the power of direct thought vibrations set in motion by your mind, which will exert a powerful effect upon the minds of others, unless they understand the secret of guarding against these forces and rendering themselves positive to others. An understanding of this law will also enable you to present a positive mental attitude toward the thought waves emanating from the minds of others.

3. By the power of the adductive qualities of thought, which works upon the theory "like attracts like." By holding certain thoughts constantly, in your mind, you attract to you thoughts and influences of the like nature, from the great body of thought surrounding us, unseen, but all powerful. This power is one of the strongest forces in nature, and if properly used will attract assistance from the most unexpected quarters. "Thoughts are Things," and possess a wonderful power of attracting to themselves other thought waves of the same vibratory pitch and quality.

4. By the power of thought in shaping your character and temperament to meet the requirements of your organization. You lack certain qualities needful for your success. You know it as well, if not better, than anyone else, but you have been deluded by a belief that these shortcomings were a part of you and that "the leopard cannot change his spots." To you the study of Para-X Powers comes as a mighty ally, for you can overcome these deficiencies, and can acquire new characteristics and qualities, as well as learning how to strengthen those which you have already. However, you must do the work yourself for every man must work out his own salvation in this study, as in every other branch of human endeavor.

The energy behind Para-X Power is the energy of Universal Creation. This energy not only permeates the entire Universe, it also flows within <u>YOU</u>. Let's demonstrate the amazing energies around Para-X Powers with six simple, yet highly demonstrative exercises to prove the POWER behind Para-X Power.

PARA-X POWERS

Exercise 1. Whilst walking down the street, fix your attention upon someone walking just ahead of you. A distance of at least six to ten feet should separate you, and a greater distance is no obstacle. Fasten a firm, steady, earnest gaze upon your subject, focusing the gaze upon the back of the neck, just at the base of the brain. Whilst gazing firmly at this point, will that the subject shall turn his head and look around in your direction. A little practice is required to perfect yourself in this exercise, but after you once acquire the "knack" of it, you will be surprised at the percentage of people whom you can affect in this way. Women seem to be more highly susceptible to this mental influence than are men.

Exercise 2. Fix your gaze upon some one sitting ahead of you in church, theater, concert, etc., focusing your gaze upon the same point as in the previous exercise, and will that the person shall look around. You will notice that the subject will fidget around in his seat, appear more or less uncomfortable, and finally half turn in his seat and direct a quick glance in your direction. This experiment will prove more successful with persons whom you know, than with strangers. The better you know the person, the quicker the influence will manifest itself. The two exercises just given can be indefinitely multiplied by the ingenuity of the student. The principle is the same in all cases, the concentrated gaze and strong, earnest, expectant willing or demanding the result, being the prime factors in producing the phenomenon. If you find difficulty in producing the above results, you will know that your powers of concentration are not sufficiently developed, and you will accordingly perfect yourself in this respect.

Exercise 3. Select some person who may be seated on the opposite side of a bus from you, but several seats to the right or left of the point directly opposite you. You may look straight ahead, so as to appear as if you were not looking at the other party, but you will be conscious of his presence, and will see him out of the corner of your eye. Direct a strong mental demand toward him, willing and expecting that he will look in your direction. If you manage it properly, you will find that in a few moments the party will suddenly glance in your direction. Sometimes the glance will be directed in a seemingly unconscious manner, just as if the party had merely felt a passing fancy to look at you, whilst in other cases the glance will be shot at you, suddenly and sharply, as if the party had been conscious of a mental call. The person obeying the call often will look embarrassed, and somewhat sheepish, when he meets your full magnetic gaze, which you have directed upon him when he turned his eyes in your direction.

Exercise 4. When talking with a person and he seems to hesitate in the choice of a word, glance sharply at him and give a strong mental suggestion of a word. In many cases he will immediately repeat the word, which you have suggested. Your word must be appropriate, as otherwise his Passive mind may hesitate about using it, and his Active mind will step in and insert another word. Some students have tried this experiment in the case of a public speaker, preacher, etc., and have related many amusing instances in their experience.

Exercise 5. An interesting experiment is that of willing the movement of a person in a certain direction. This can be tried when walking behind a person on the street, by focusing the gaze as instructed. When the person approaches another person walking in the opposite direction, you may will the subject to turn either to the right or left, in passing the other person. You may also try this experiment in the case of a person approaching you in the street. In this case you should walk straight ahead, turning neither to the right nor to the left, keeping your gaze fixed on the approaching party, and making a mental command that he turn to the right or left, as you will.

Exercise 6. Stand at your window and fix your eyes upon an approaching person, at the same time willing that he turn his head and look at you while passing. You will find that he will obey your mental attraction, seven times out of ten, providing your powers of concentration are sufficiently well developed. Even without the practice of the Concentrations exercises, you will be able to influence passer by sufficiently often to satisfy you that there is "something in it." You will be able to obtain better results in this particular experiment, if you will stand at a first floor window rather than at a window higher from the ground. The motion of obeying the impulse and merely turning the head being so much easier than the motion of looking up to a second or third floor window, the percentage of results obtained by the first plan will greatly exceed those of the latter one. This exercise may be varied by the plan of compelling the attention of a person seated at a window, which you are passing, and so on. When you once begin to practice these exercises, you will find it so fascinating that you will invent new plans of testing your power, you being governed by the particular circumstances of the occasion.

These exercises not only show you the POWER behind Para-X Power, they also will do much to develop confidence in you powers, and to aid you in acquiring the "knack' of sending out the vibratory impulses. They are of course more or less trifling in their natures, and unworthy of the exercise of the mental powers, except as a means of practice.

They should not be used merely for the amusement of the student, and never for the amusement of his friends. One should never trifle with these mighty forces, nor exhibit them for the gratification of the vulgar curiosity of others. Para-X Powers should always be used responsibly and never to hurt or harm others.

LIKE ATTRACTS LIKE

The character of the thought vibrations sent out by us depends upon the nature of the thought itself. If thought had color (and some say that they have), we should see our fear and worry thought as murky, heavy, clouds hanging close to the earth; our bright, cheerful and happy, confident, 'I can and I will' thought as light, fleecy, vapory clouds hanging close to the earth; our bright, cheerful and happy, confident, "I can and I Will" thoughts as light, fleecy, vapory clouds, traveling swiftly and mingling with others of their kind, forming fleecy cloud banks, high above the "I can't" thoughts.

No matter how far your thought waves may travel, they retain a certain connection with you and exert an influence over you as well as others. You cannot easily get rid of the influence over you as well as others. You cannot easily get rid of the influence of these "children of your mind." If you have been sending out bad thoughts, you are subject to their influence, and your only hope is to neutralize and counteract them by sending out strong, new thought waves of the proper sort, or by asserting the I AM, and thereby creating a mental aura, or by both means.

The old saying "Like attracts like" and "Birds of a feather flock together," are both literally exemplified by the tendencies of thought waves. There is what is known as the "Adductive Quality of Thought," the word "adductive" being derived from the Latin word adductum, to bring to. The manifestation of this quality of thought is one of the most wonderful features in the realm of Para-X Powers.

Good thought attracts good – evil thoughts, evil. If you hate a man and send him your hate thoughts, you will get hate in return, and will face a hating and hateful world. In the thought world, you get back what you send out – with interest. Send out kind thoughts and kind thoughts will return to you, with compound interest, and you will find yourself greeted by a kind, helping world.

It really does pay to think the best thoughts. If you will practice thinking along these lines for one month, you will find the greatest difference in your life. Before the month will have passed you will be conscious of the helpful force of the responsive thought waves, and your life will seem entirely different to you. Try it now, you will never regret it.

HOW TO MAKE MORE MONEY

If you want to make more money, then you have to closely follow this method. This is called "The Self-Written Check." A self-written check is one in which you will write your own name on the "pay to" line and with the amount of money you desire. Now let us discuss the step-by-step method which will result in making more money or the amount of money that you desire.

Determine The Sum Of Money You Desire: Just remember the equation that "thought + emotion = attraction." Keep in mind the formula and write down the amount of money desired by you, on a check, and look at it every day. Make the amount on the check exciting so that the law of attraction works in a better way for you. If your desire and excitement are strong enough, you will get the money faster and with more ease.

Pen The Check: The second step is to write the check. Fill in a blank check with the amount of money you desire. Write your name and fill in the date when you want to receive the money. Make the whole situation as real as you can possibly make it.

Keep On Looking At The Check For As Long As Possible Until You Get The Money You Desire: Keep the check clean and in a place where you can see it whenever you want to see it. Handle the check with care. I would advise you to keep the check in your work place so that you can look at it whenever you want to look at it.

Now make use of this simple method of self-written check and make the law of attraction work for you. You will make the sum of money that you desire.

If you want to make more money by using Para-X Power, then you need to center your emotion, thought and visualization in that direction. Be specific with your requirements, as the law of attraction will work faster only when you know what you want in particular. For example, you want to go on a vacation. Think that you are already on your day off and in the place where you want to be. Imagine that you are having fun with your family and friends at the spot where you wanted to be.

But remember that thinking about what you want is not enough. You have to feel the emotion that you will get when you have what you desire. Get into the feeling deep down and indulge yourself in your imagination. Feel the same way you would feel when you have the money. You have to imagine that your bank balance is showing the amount of money you desired. See that this thought comes to you regularly, consciously or unconsciously.

The most powerful way to unleash your millionaire mind and to invoke Para-X Power is by being grateful. Gratitude is a very powerful feeling which can do wonders. Here are three keys which can open the locks of your financial success.

A Well-Defined Objective: Have a clear objective of actually how much you want in numerical terms. If you are going in for investments, then have in your mind the percentage of returns you are looking for. It can be 5%, 10% or even 25%. The only thing is that you must have a realistic 'rate of return' objective. This will assist you to focus on the objective, and you can plan accordingly. You take decisions to achieve the target.

Your Mental Attitude Should Be Positive: Always have a positive attitude on whatever you do. Always be positive in whatever target you want to reach in your financial holdings. Think and start living in that environment of achievement. Draw your plans accordingly. This will give you peace of mind and your attitude will automatically be positive.

Plan Your Goal: Planning is the most crucial part of your achievements. You can accomplish only if you have well-charted plans. Without plans, you will be lost in an unknown place, from which you will have no way out. Investments without plans will take you nowhere. So always have ideal and realistic plans before venturing.

Some people believe that using the power of positive thinking will surely manifest cash. Even though they are not completely wrong, the positive attitude is just one step in the correct way. Bear in mind that positive thinking alone, or the law of attraction alone, will not help you improve your financial position.

Your positive attitude along with Para-X Power is only a tool. You have to make use of the tool to manifest the conditions that will make you wealthy. The tool will not create the wealth itself, but it will help you achieve your goal.

The thought that you have is the origin of your asset and it assists in making things happen. Your thoughts directly shape your power to attract wealth. You must be aware of your thoughts. Only healthy awareness will bring about the change that you want.
You must have choice and decision linked with a firm dedication to act. Change yourself to be aware of the effect of your thoughts. Finally, your habits will determine your wealthy lifestyle, which in turn will help you to improve your financial position.

The energy behind Para-X Power is the energy of Universal Creation. This energy not only permeates the entire Universe, it also flows within YOU.

PARA-X POWERS

CAN THERE REALLY BE "MONEY FROM NOTHING?"

There is a skill to establishing money. When you realize the essence of money at its finer, smaller-than-atomic level, you will understand that you are never hapless. It does not take wealth to create wealth.

You must start to see money opportunities everywhere. You should become aware as to how money moves from one hand to another. Once you understand this, you will become confident and more skilled to attract money towards you. This does not require any technical education on your part. You need not invest large amounts of money.

Here are some basic steps to help you make money from nothing:

The first step is that you must center your thoughts on money. Imagine that money is your friend. Love money as you would love your friend. However, do not be greedy for money. Because greed will result only in tension and nothing else. Form a healthy love for money. Try to meditate on money for at least thirty minutes every day. Visualize actual money in your hands. Imagine that you have more money and you are living a happy life.

The second step is to wipe out debts. You will have to see that all your bills and the debts that you owe are paid promptly. Once you are relieved of the bill tensions, you can center your thoughts on making money in abundance.

The next step is to chart out your monthly income and expenditures. Prepare a budget that you can handle. This way you can cut all your unnecessary expenditures.

The fourth step is to reduce your unnecessary expenditures. For example, you make a list before you go to a shop to buy things. This will help you buy only those things that you want, and you can keep your hands away from unwanted things.

Try to step up your income. You can achieve this by either working for more hours at your present job, or by taking up extra work. You can also try your hand at making multiple streams of income.

Since you have cut down your unnecessary expenses and raised your income, now you can save your money. Try to save as much as possible every month.

The final step is to be thankful. Look at the money you have and be thankful that you have at least this much. This will help you to expand your views.

As we have said throughout this book: whatever you attract into your life will be pulled towards you because of the law of attraction. When you think or feel, some vibrations are given off from your body. Your vibrations may be positive or negative. When your thoughts are happy, your vibrations are positive. But when your thoughts are sad, your vibrations are negative.

The vibration of your thoughts can be used to make money. Vibrations will determine how fast and how well you can manifest what you need. The feeling inside you is always changing. You can use this vibration to your advantage to unleash the law of attraction.

The key to success is your high vibration. A feeling of fear engulfs you when you know that you have not paid your bills. This will lower your vibrations. And you will not be able to manifest what you want when your vibration is low. The lower your vibration, the lower will be your ability to think positively. If you want to make the law of attraction work for you, then you have to raise your vibration and maintain it at a high level.

Here are some tips to increase your vibration: *You Have To Visualize About The Things You Want In Your Life Every Day.* Every morning spend at least 10 minutes imagining what you want in life. This will really work wonders for you. Make this a habit. This will increase your visualization capacity. This increased capacity of visualization in you will help you to attract things towards you at a faster pace. If you are able to add your emotion to your visualization, you will get the things you want faster.

Pay More Attention To Your Emotions. Just keep track of when your emotion falls and when it rises. If you are able to know this, you can easily and quickly fix your energy level. If your vibration falls only a bit, you can easily increase it. But if your energy level falls significantly, then it will be very difficult for you to bring it up.

Music Also Affects Your Vibration. Change the type of music that you listen to. Only listen to those types of music which will help you to increase your vibrations. Discover the music that produces the palpitation inside you, which is in conjunction with what you are attempting to pull to yourself.

Vibrations also depend on the food which we take in every day. Fast food, which is very heavy, does not create high vibrations. Vegetarian meals help you to maintain higher vibrations. The water that you drink can create vibration. Just charge the water that you are drinking with some intention. This charge will increase your vibration. Charging your drinking water can be done by saying a prayer. After you practice this with your drinking water, try it with the food you eat. This will charge you with positive vibrations.

The truth about Para-X Powers is that once you know of its existence, you want to master it. But the actual fact is that you are already a master of this power. Whatever you have in your life now is the result of Para-X Power. Now the important issue is not how to master the attractor factor, but you should be able to master it so that you attract whatever you desire.

The law of attraction along with Para-X Power has existed since time immemorial. The law has been working in your life since your earliest moments. The law is standard and it cannot change. The only variable factor in the law is you. So make sure that you change to utilize the law in your life. The more you change, the more you will get the things into your life which you want.

Things in your life will start changing only if you begin to change. The notion that Para-X Power will attract things in your life when you know about it is only a fairy tale. Things will change only if you change. If you want the things you desire, then you should visualize that you already have them. One of the most crucial things that you must realize is that using Para-X Power requires action on your part. If you keep this in mind, you will achieve all that you desire.

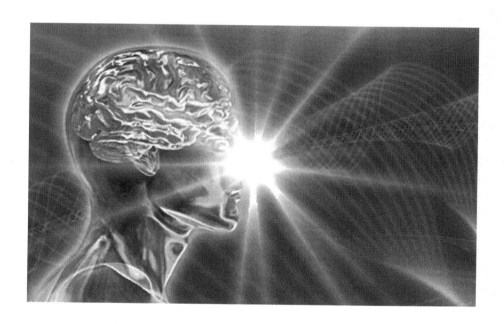

PARA-X POWERS

Write for our <u>FREE</u> Catalog:

Global Communications
P.O. Box 753
New Brunswick, NJ 08903

Email: mrufo8@hotmail.com

Visit our website at:

www.conspiracyjournal.com

Made in the USA
Charleston, SC
13 July 2012